Reflections:
Grimoire of a Modern Witch

BY
MARIA 'PEACOCK' BARRETT

Copyright © 2016 by Maria 'Peacock' Barrett
All rights reserved.

Green Ivy Publishing
1 Lincoln Centre
18W140 Butterfield Road
Suite 1500
Oakbrook Terrace IL 60181-4843
www.greenivybooks.com

ISBN: 978-1-945650-35-2

Table of Contents

Dedication	VI
Introduction	VII
Deity and the Elements	1
Gods and Goddesses	2
The Devil	4
The Elements	5
Making Spirituality Personal	9
Deity Exercise:	14
Elements of a Ritual	16
Intent	16
Location	16
Constructing the Ceremony	17
Creating Sacred Space	18
Visualization Exercise:	18
Casting a Circle	22
Altar Exercise:	25
Cleansing and Anointing	27
Calling the Quarters	28
Earth	29
Water	30
Air	32
Fire	33
Invocation of the God and Goddess	36
The Goddess	37
The God	39
A Beltane Ritual	42
Closing the Circle	46
Ritual Exercise	47
Life Stages & Celebrations - The Wheel of the Year	55
Yule	56
Creation	59
Wiccaning	61

Candelmas	67
Petitioning	69
Oestara	71
Coming of Age	73
Initiation	77
Beltane	81
The Great Rite	82
Hand-fasting	85
Litha	89
Healing	91
Lughnasaad (Lammas)	95
Communion	96
Mabon	100
Croning and Saging	100
Thanksgiving	102
Samhain	105
Tolerance	107
On Living and Dying	112
Rebirth Ceremony	116
Life Lessons—Honing the Craft	121
Moon Magick	121
Skills of the Craft	131
Facing Fears	132
Weaving Focus	137
Mirror Gazing	141
Vision Questing	144
Forgiveness	146
Conclusion	153
References	156
Suggested Author List	157
Resources	158

Dedication

This book is dedicated to my father, the Writer, and my mother, the Dreamer. It is also dedicated to my daughter, Tiffany, and my sons, T. J. and Zachary. They are a reflection of the best of me, showing me things through their eyes that I wouldn't see on my own, and keeping me young while sharing their wisdom with me. To my lover and partner, Todd, I thank you from the bottom of my heart. You are my treasure and I wouldn't be the same whole, happy woman I am today without you in my life. You stood by me during this process and never questioned, and you've taught me what unconditional love is all about!

To my family and friends, my brothers and sisters in spirit, and those who have only just placed their feet on this path, I offer this work for your consideration. In sharing it, I have shared myself.

Blessed Be!

Introduction

I come from a land where the elves dwell in shadowy glades of tall-standing trees.
They gather under the Sun with smiles and laughter, playing musical tones that tickle the senses, singing the songs of times gone by and times yet to come.
They gather under the moon with mystery and delight, playing drums that echo the heartbeat of the land, dancing the primal rhythm of the Earth that is deep within their soul.
They commune with Nature, walking sky-clad under a bright blue heaven, seeing pictures in the puffy white clouds or feeling the rains that wash over them, cleansing and renewing them.
They eat and drink and they are merry, thankful for the bounties of grape and grain that the Mother and Father have provided.
They worship, celebrate, love, and submit to themselves and each other so that they can grow, learn, feel, and activate that which is divine within and without.
For they are the Elves, Guardians of Nature and the Secrets of Life.

Today I am an Elf and a Wiccan Priestess.
I revere the elements of Nature and have a personal connection to the Divine Creator.
I gather under the Sun with smiles and laughter.
I gather under the Moon to share the mysteries in delight.
I walk sky-clad under a bright blue heaven.
I eat, drink, and am very merry.
I worship, love, celebrate, and submit.
I come from a land where the Elves dwell and I am one of them.
My name is Peacock and this is my story.

I was raised in the suburbs, all clean matching houses in a neighborhood with 2.6 kids in every home and a car in every garage. This was definitely a contradiction to the lifestyle that my family lived. My parents were what you'd refer to as hippies. They raised us in a home with open doors and open minds. We vacationed in nature; camping and canoeing were our two primary forms of recreation. These events shaped my perceptions and memories, my habits and hobbies, and I, too, became a hippie. Not a big surprise, I guess. We are, after all, a product of our environment in many ways.

I went to my first Pagan gathering in 1989. Being of an open mind, I attended a "festival for alternative thinkers" in the middle of the woods that a friend of mine had recommended. I had always been fascinated with Nature, with alternative living, and with exploration of new thoughts and ideas. Why not explore this new adventure?

Lothlorien Nature Sanctuary[1] is located in the hills of southern Indiana and is named after a forest where the Elves dwell in Tolkien's Lord of the Rings series. It was formed by four earthly individuals with a divine idea: to create a space of worship, education, and activation for those who believed that there were alternative ways to live, love, and express faith while paying tribute to the Earth. It was here that I was exposed to Wicca for the first time.

I felt frustrated with the major religions I had experienced. None of them seemed to call to me in any special way. There was no connection between my Creator and me. There was no question that I *believed*, but what did I believe? How could I make that belief a real factor in my life instead of an abstract concept saved for Sundays and Christmas?

What Wicca offered was the answer for me. It helped me to honor life and have respect for myself, for others, for all living creatures, and for the Earth as a living entity. It also helped me find harmony. Internally, I have the knowledge that I need to look no further than inside myself to find that which is sacred, and externally I know that I am linked to everything that the Divine has created. I have been a Wiccan priestess for twenty-five years now, and as I reflect on the person that I am today, I

---

1 For more information, visit www.elvinhome.org.

can say that I am closer to my Creator than ever before.

Seeking faith and a greater purpose in life is a common bond that all mankind shares. That path is as individual as each of us, like a snowflake falling from the sky. I have chosen to share my journey because sometimes you just need a road map. I share my lessons because I think that all paths into the Light teach us some fundamental things about life and faith that are Universal. I share because I want to be part of the collective consciousness in a real and meaningful way. And I share to give thanks and praise to the Lord and Lady for the many blessings that have been bestowed upon me while traveling the path to enlightenment.

While preparing to venture off to my twenty-third Elf Fest, a coworker asked me,

"Oh, do you practice when you go there?"

My answer was polite. I touted the virtues of maypole dancing, fire pit drumming, workshops, and vending.

But my real response is this: Practicing Magick is the same as practicing any other religion. Being a practicing Wiccan, Christian, Muslim, or Jew doesn't mean that you reserve your beliefs for those moments in church or on holidays. Believing in something is an ongoing process, a set of daily rules to live by, a greater power to pray to, to call upon in happy times and bad, and to thank and revere always. We are the physical manifestation of that which is within us, the spark of the divine that is our very spirit. It is our duty to represent our Creator with pride and confidence, love and honesty, peace and grace. This is the greatest honor we can pay to them and to all living kind.

Anyone who puts forth the time and effort it takes to write an entire book must have many things persuading them to do so. Of course, we all have goals for personal success. Some seek the fame, recognition, and money that would accompany a bestselling novel. Some tell tales of suspense or adventure, mystery or fantasy to entertain, taking the mind to far-off or imaginary places, taking readers outside of everyday life and allowing them to dream of other realities. Some seek to grow from the experience after having researched some topic, profession, or theme and then expounding on that knowledge through writing about it and sharing it with others. Others want to be known for making a mark in this life, contributing to the greater good of mankind in some small way. I can confess that I have a little of all of these motivating me.

Mostly though, I want to share my experiences and lessons with my family, who has not always understood my path. I want to share them with my children and their children, and theirs . . . so they can avoid some of the pitfalls of life and spiritual seeking, and so they can look back at their ancestral line with understanding, pride, and a sense of belonging. But I also want to share my experiences with the world, to influence even some small portion of humanity to seek a greater truth. We are part of the Collective Consciousness, connected on a spiritual level to every other human being on this planet and to the planet itself. We each have a place in the world that is uniquely held by us and each of us has a destiny as a Magickal Being to realize our part in making it a better place. In gaining a global awareness of our interconnectivity, and the impact our actions and thought-forms have on others and Mother Earth, we can manifest a world of communication and education, of sustainability, of helping and healing, of peace and love. I think, ultimately, writing this book has been a calling for me as I'm sure it is with any author. When the words won't be silent until they are allowed to be free, to be shared by others, then it is a calling that cannot be ignored!

As the Grateful Dead would say, "What a long strange trip it's been!"

Best wishes on your journey down the spiritual path! May it be your best trip yet!

Deity and the Elements

In beginning to write about my spiritual journey, I find it important and necessary to define my spiritual beliefs and practices as a point of reference for anything which may follow in this book. After I had attended my first couple of Pagan festivals, my dad, who was in part responsible for formulating my personality as an open-minded seeker, accused me of involving my children and myself in something I knew little to nothing about. Partly out of concern for my children, and partly to prove him wrong, I went about reading as many books as I could get my hands on about Paganism, Wicca, and ancient world religions and traditions. As I began to gather knowledge, I became more convinced than ever that I had stumbled on something that lit a flame in me where other paths of enlightenment had failed to light a spark. With that in mind, I began to sort through the different traditions in Paganism to find the right path for me.

For many years now, I have been—in the general meaning of the term—a self-declared Pagan. More specifically, I practice what is referred to as Wicca. This makes me Wiccan and means that you can call me a "Witch" in the modern-day definition of the word. One of the reasons I chose this path was that there was no one book to follow, no hierarchy of individuals that I had to honor, and no prescription for how it *must* be done. But now I had to determine what exactly I did and didn't believe as part of the growing process in adopting this new faith. With such a large umbrella of a term, I hoped to narrow down some tenets that seemed to fit with the new form of spirituality that I was going to practice.

No matter which path each of us may take to enlightenment, we choose to believe certain truths and practice certain rituals according to the tenets of that faith. For many people, it may involve attending church on a regular basis, praying to a singular God figure or trinity of figures, for intercession with the problems of daily life, for healing or wisdom, and/or for miracles. It may involve communing with others of the same religious beliefs and practices to which they subscribe. It may have a recognizable, organized, and political system of hierarchy amongst its most senior or important members. It may include adherence to a certain set of moral codes. It may also include a representation of Evil, or sin incarnate, referred to as Satan, or the devil.

Gods and Goddesses

Wiccans also have certain tenets, or beliefs. These are similar across different Wiccan traditions and best describe the beliefs to which I subscribe. I believe in the sanctity of all living things and of the planet itself, known as Gaia, or Mother Earth. I also believe that religion is polytheistic in nature. This means that I believe the Divine Creator can be represented by one or more entities that can be female and/or male. In the Wiccan tradition, this balance, or duality of deity, is commonly represented by the "Lord and Lady" or the "God and Goddess." This duality can be seen represented in all aspects of existence and is obvious when reviewing the following: Male/Female (masculine/feminine), Young/Old, Right/Wrong, In/Out, Happy/Sad, Healthy/Sick, Yin/Yang, Good/Evil, and Within/Without. The Creator can also be represented by a pantheon, a group of these beings that can be assigned to different aspects of human existence and nature.

Throughout history, mankind has worshipped archetypes that represent God, the One, the Creator, the Divine. These images were, and are, created to give some corporeal aspects to something that is unimaginable, indescribable, and otherworldly. When studying the Celts, the Romans and Grecians, the Egyptians, the Vikings, the Chinese, the Aborigines, and the Native Americans, you will find that Gods and Goddesses have been worshipped as either Supreme Beings or as archetypes that represent certain aspects of human existence and interaction. These images allowed people to bring the unknowable into a realm that they could understand. In Greek mythology for instance, an entire hierarchy of Gods and Goddesses were worshipped from 1500 BC to AD 500. They were believed to be created by two primordial deities, Cronus (the child of Gaia,

Mother Earth, and Uranus Father of the Titans) and his sister, and consort, Rhea. They, in turn gave birth to Zeus, supreme ruler of the universe, and Zeus's wife and consort, Hera. These deities were the progenitors of the many Demi-Gods and Demi-Goddesses, each of which represented some aspect of humanity. The following is a list of some of them and the aspects over which they ruled:

Kore (Goddess) represented agriculture, farming, and animal husbandry

Helios (God) represented the sky, sun, and all astral bodies

Ares (God) represented war and battles

Demeter (Goddess) represented fertility and vegetation

Hephaestus (God) represented fire and smith crafting

Artemis (Goddess) represented fishing and hunting

Aphrodite (Goddess) represented love and sex

Hermes (God) was the messenger of the Gods

Daphne (Goddess) was an oracle who could see past, present, and future

Logos (God) represented logic and reason

Poseidon (God) represented the oceans, seas, and all aquatic creatures

Pluto (God) represented wealth

Dionysus (God) represented wine, grape, and grain, and the harvest [1]

As you can see, this is a very long list of deity figures that were worshipped for nearly two thousand years. Each of these deities had temples built in their honor and ceremonies and holidays that they ruled over. These deities were called upon

---

[1] Michael Jordan; 1993/Encyclopedia of Gods – pg. 307-8/ Facts on File, Inc.

for intervention during the everyday lives of the peoples who worshipped them. This was mankind's attempt at placing human aspects within the hands of supernatural or omnipotent beings and was no less valid to them than are any of the God figures we worship today.

In modern Wicca, the God(s) and Goddess(es) are called upon as Supreme deities who have the powers of intervention and blessing on our lives. As such, we view these past deities as valid archetypes still, for they are not the actual deities that we call upon, but rather the representatives of the One. Thus, I have called upon archetypes from many different faiths, both current and past, to preside over my rituals and bring my thanks and wishes for the future to the One, the Creator, the Divine.

The Devil

I do NOT believe in a central figure known as Satan or in any supernatural individual or group of individuals (i.e., demons or evil spirits) that can cause us to do evil against our will. I also do not believe in the concept of original sin that is common to the Judeo-Christian belief system. I believe that at the center of each of us lies a soul or spirit that *is* The Divine, existing as pure energy and directly linked to the Creator. As divine beings, we have the ability to tap into and harness the creative and infinite power of the Universe in a personal and intimate way. This means that we have the ability to make choices based on our own beliefs of right or wrong. It also means that we are responsible for our own actions and reactions to people, circumstances, and things that we encounter in our lives. One of my favorite quotes reads,

"Bad as he is, the devil may be abused, be falsely charged and causelessly accused when Man, unwilling to be blamed alone, shift off those crimes on Him that are their own."[2]

We cannot blame any creature such as Satan for our bad decision making, lack of regard for others, or self-promoting

---

[2] Tony Willis;1988/ Magick and the Tarot: Using Tarot to Manipulate the Unseen Forces of the Universe – pg. 67/ HarperCollins Publishing

agendas. We can't blame outside forces for "bad luck" or unfortunate circumstances. We must accept ownership for our lives and the paths that we choose for good or bad. This is not to say that bad things don't happen to good people. As we know, natural disasters affect many people around the globe on a daily basis, as do physical and mental illness, poverty, famine, war, genocide, homelessness, crimes, abuse, and discrimination of all forms. This *is* to say that we have a direct impact on how we choose to handle the situations that present themselves in life. Always remember, when making choices, we hold within us the ability to "seek the light" and rise to any challenge with Divine power.

Integral to the Wiccan belief system is also a belief in reincarnation. While recognizing a place similar to Heaven, known as the Summerland to some, we recognize no such place as Hell or purgatory. I believe, as do some, that the Summerland is an ethereal place of peace and reflection where our souls have a chance to regroup and connect with the Divine. It affords us the opportunity to examine our next life, what purpose it will hold, and what impact on the human experience we may have. I call this phase of the reincarnation process "mission identification." Finally, our soul is reborn to the physical world again during the moment of conception between and man and a woman.

The Elements

I also believe in the Elements of nature, Earth, Water, Air, Fire, and the fifth, element, Ether (also Aether), and their interrelationship with our existence as human beings. Each Element can be represented by many things in the physical world that are also associated with that particular Element. These Elementals, or symbols of the Element themselves, include the plants, rock formations, water features, and vast array of creatures found occurring in Nature itself, along with the Earth and all the Heavenly bodies that make up our Universe. In practice, we can represent these Elements in a variety of ways and for a variety of reasons.

These range from placing knickknacks around the home

or garden as gentle reminders of our connection to the Divine to using symbolic items as a way of creating sacred space and performing religious rites and ceremonies.

The first of these Elements, Earth, represents the physical side of existence and is the first that we must all master as human beings. We start as infants, with no ability to fend for ourselves, and must learn to walk, eat, speak, use the restroom, clothe ourselves, bathe and brush our hair and teeth, and avoid dangers like fire, traffic, angry dogs, schoolyard bullies, and household poisons in order to exist in the physical world. We also learn to work, put a roof over our head, transport ourselves to various places, and participate in society and commerce. Earth represents the physical body, physical health and fitness, stability and a firm foundation, physical labor, work, money and finance, home, hearth, and family, planting, reaping and all farming, forestry, and animal husbandry. As a seeker of higher consciousness, let me say that if you do not have mastery of this first element in your life, you will find exploration of the elements that follow more challenging. That doesn't mean that it is impossible, just that survival can occupy a lot of your time if you don't have your Earthly affairs in order.

The second Element is Water and represents our emotional existence and experiences. As human beings, we are aware of emotion as early as birth, as the importance of maternal bonding will show. We express our confusion in emotional terms from early on in life, far before verbal communication becomes a skill that will help us express our feelings more clearly. We feel love, anger, joy, sorrow, and an infinite number of other emotions, and we begin by expressing them through tears, laughter, hugs, and screams before we can finally put into words *what* we are feeling. Water represents the heart, the blood, and circulatory system, but also gentle healing, nurturing, love, friendship, and all matters of the heart. It also represents art, music, literature, dance, and all creative endeavors that are spawned by emotion. Emotions can be almost as strong a motivating factor as survival if we allow them to rule our judgment and logic. But, in balance, decisions made from the heart are not always bad. In fact, love and compassion are two of the things that separate us from other living creatures along with the ability to feel friendship and connectivity to other human beings. This is one of the things that makes us sacred.

Air is the third Element and represents the intellectual, logical side of human existence. It also represents that which is unseen but exists at the subconscious level. The brain, the nervous system, and the id, ego, and superego are ruled by Air. It also represents dreaming, intuition, instinct, psychic ability, second sight, and premonition/precognition. As human beings, this journey begins when we start to associate speech with logical, predictable results. If/then and action/consequence soon follow as we grow as intelligent beings. We begin to understand communication, mathematics, science, and the abstract ideas of time and space as relative to our existence. We use knowledge from a variety of fields of study as a tool for greater efficiency in living and progressing as a species. To us, this is logical and beneficial. We begin to perceive that there is wisdom that only comes with time and experience. We can also grasp some awareness that is not clear to the conscious mind but that exists as thought patterns nonetheless. We perceive things throughout our lives that are unseen, from déjà vu moments that become real in the future to things that can only be described as "gut feelings," guided by intuition, premonition, or what some call "psychic" awareness.

Learning to open the mind's eye is one of the focuses of the journey through Air. It is estimated that as humans, we use approximately 10 percent of our brains for logical, active thinking while the other 90 percent is active in other endeavors like memory storage, recording your surroundings, listening to background noise as you hold a conversation, etc . . . Learning to engage your subconscious mind in meaningful and useful ways is one of the "tricks" of Magick. It allows you the ability to engage 100 percent of your effort, purpose, and intent into manifesting your desired goals or effecting change. We will discuss this more in the coming pages.

Fire is the next Element on the list. It is the passion that drives procreation, the primal desire to continue the species through creating human life. It is the lust we feel when we meet someone we are attracted to and our hormones rage. It is the moment of climax, when fireworks explode and we are transported beyond the physical into the Light. It represents Spirit and is the spark of creation that is needed to produce something from nothing. It is the "What If" moment that precedes the action to make anything happen. It is the idea that takes form and becomes reality, the sword that is created from raw materials with heat and pressure, until it is honed into a masterpiece. As human beings, we begin our journey through fire when we accomplish the first task that we thought was impossible or feel the jolt of electricity when we cross the finish line and experience victory. The first moment for many of us probably came when we "let go" and took our first independent step. It was our first lesson in faith. We believed that we could let go and make *it* happen, *the impossible*, for the first time, and we did it! This moment of "faith realized" happens each time we try something new and succeed, whether it be through renewed faith in ourselves or through faith in a Divine outside source or Creator. Once we understand that *we* can create, that we can make something from nothing and be the start of something bigger than ourselves, we begin to ask ourselves questions like,

Is there a God and if so, am I part of some "Great Design"? or Why am I here, and what impact am I going to have on this planet?

This seeking, or quest if you will, exists across the human experience, no matter what God you believe in or what faith you practice.

The fifth Element, the hardest to define or quantify, is sometimes referred to as "Ether" (Aether) and exists as the "soul" of each human being. It is the indefinable part of each of us that *is* the Creator in pure form, linked perfectly and forever with the Divine. It exists as pure energy and as such, cannot be destroyed, only redistributed into other forms as it changes and adapts to the universe. Some believe that this form of energy can travel outside the body (astrally) to explore other places and/or realities. Some believe that the Soul can manifest itself as angel, ghost, or vision after our death. Still others believe that the moment of reincarnation is more instantaneous than that, or that the Souls in the Summerland cannot be reached from the living world. I tend to believe that all of these are possibilities. After all, Thank Gods, I have never been dead, at least in this incarnation, so I can really only speculate. This is one of the reasons we as human beings become seekers on a spiritual journey. Not only do we want to figure out our purpose in this life, but we want to know what lies beyond it and whether there is really something greater out there than the sum of our lives as finite dots on a timeline.

One of the other logics that rings true from this Element is that the existence of Original Sin or the concept that we are all flawed and need to be fixed somehow along our spiritual path is inherently wrong. For if we "listen" to the soul at our deepest selves, we cannot help but find the Divine within us, waiting for us to harness the power of pure thought, love, and peace to guide us along our way as we seek the truths that can be known and understood by all.

Making Spirituality Personal

As I adopted this alternate framework for worship involving ritual, celebration, meditation, and prayer, I read many books on the subject of Modern Wicca. I also learned about many ancient traditions and religions, and the Gods and Goddesses recognized throughout the history of mankind in a myriad of cultures and across eons of time. Each seemed to be a search for knowledge, an attempt to rise up to challenges with belief and with a connectivity to the Divine. Each required a leap of faith and was based on the world around them as mirrored, or even amplified, by the Deities of their particular faith and practice.

One aspect of Wicca that appealed to me was that there seemed to be no "wrong" way to practice it. There was no specific

"Bible," per se, that needed to be adhered to or referenced in times of difficulty or when in need of inspiration. The ceremonies, rituals, poems, and prayers were not predetermined and seemed to be tailored to the needs of the individual or group that was participating in the process at the time. The "faithful" participants of these activities reached into ancient cultures and religions, into traditional and modern mythos and fairy tales, and plucked that which best represented their needs, whether they be celebratory in nature or to seek intervention from the Divine, and created something new that was real and meaningful to them. These rituals, ceremonies, writings, musings, and prayers, and their end results, seen and felt by the participants and by myself through years of practice and belief, have been as real to me as any that I experienced when I was growing up and being told what to believe or how I should practice that belief.

The Bible, as an example, is certainly a book filled with wisdom and life lessons. It is one of many books from our past that contains valuable information and mythology that can still be useful today in teaching us things such as forgiveness, love, tolerance, and faith in something greater than ourselves. It is, in fact, a book I have used many times for provoking thought and as a source of inspiration. But I have found that while the tenets of all the world's positive religions are similar, the manner in which they are practiced seems very dictatorial and monochromatic. Adherence to certain beliefs and practices are "requirements" of membership and guilt or "sin" is assigned to those who think "outside the box" or fail to follow the guidelines set forth by the "church" or governing organization.

To me, this didn't foster an individual connection with the Divine, rather it limited the experience that I felt I was "allowed" to have with my Creator. Within the frame that is Wicca, and by following the Wheel of the Year, I could adapt my rituals, prayers, and celebrations to mean something personal and transformative in my life. In the many years that I have been a Witch, I have meditated, celebrated, performed ceremonies, and uttered prayers that were based on spirituality from around the globe and across time, selecting the tradition, pantheon, or intent that was important or meaningful to me at the time. As a priestess of Wicca, I have done the same when presiding over rituals and ceremonies designed to benefit the group of participants in the activity as well as for victims of tragedies and natural disasters, or mankind and the planet as a whole. I have been a witness to miracles, or Magick, if you will, that have astounded me and left me to believe without a doubt that individualized worship can and does work!

So where does one begin? Well, the fact that you are reading this book means that you have already begun seeking spirituality as part of your human experience. I might guess that you have found some disconnect in the belief system that was presented to you in your formative years (if any) and that you are looking for a different, more expansive, more personally meaningful set of beliefs and practices than those you are currently familiar with. Let me say that no two journeys are the same; each person by the very fact of their individuality will have a wholly unique experience with the Divine even if they share the same religious belief system and practices as another. I will also say that if you seek this Divine connection with sincerity, truth, and love, then you will always find your feet on the right path, wherever it may lead. Listening to the Creator within, you will make the correct choices for yourself or find that, when you have decided incorrectly, course correction will come more easily when you link yourself to the Divine within and listen to what It is telling you.

In the following chapters, you will find a how-to of sorts that lays out the basics of creating sacred space and holding ceremonies around the Wheel of the Year. You will also find examples of many ceremonies (or parts thereof) that I have personally written and used over my twenty-five years of practicing Magick. I relate them to you not as a set of rules or ceremonies that must be recreated exactly or recited from memory but as a springboard for ideas on how *you* might create your own unique, meaningful religious experience. I have also included chapter exercises to help you define how you would like to connect with the Gods and Goddesses. Like anything worth achieving, leading a spiritual life takes work. However, I think you will find that it is a labor of love, of yourself and others as well as Mother Earth and the Universe as a whole.

Remember that there is no wrong way of "doing it" as long as your heart, mind, and intent are filled with love and positivity. Also remember that as humans, we make mistakes. When mistakes occur, and they will, these are not fatal errors that spoil or nullify your intent. Rather than letting frustration, discouragement, or guilt get the better of you, laugh at your mistakes and move on. Laughter is the best way to handle any error, real or perceived, in the process of worship and is felt in the ripples of the Collective Consciousness as positive energy. Begin again, where you left off, and finish what you started. No one likes a quitter!

Deciding to delve into alternative spirituality is a big undertaking. You will find that obstacles exist in many forms. You may encounter internal pressure from yourself as you replay the "tapes" that echo in your head from your childhood, telling you what is the "right" or "wrong" way to worship. Always listen to your deepest soul in matters of spiritual "right" and "wrong." As human beings, we instinctively know when we are doing something that is harmful to us. If your intent is pure, honest, and loving, you can trust that your internal alarm system will be clanging loudly if you are delving into something you shouldn't be. Listen to your alarm system and follow the path that makes you feel whole, content, and uplifted.

You may encounter pressure from family when you begin to practice a religion that is not in line with their teaching or beliefs, especially if you come from a family with a very strict spiritual and moral background. They may be deeply hurt if you choose to shy away from traditional religious practices and adherences. They may even find it hard to forgive you or may be truly afraid that you are putting your soul at risk. It is because they love and care about you that they show concern, anger, or an unwillingness to understand. Know that this is your choice, not theirs, and try to be understanding, patient, and loving. Also, remember that your new spiritual choice does not require you to wave a spiritual "flag" declaring your newfound enlightenment for the world to see. If you wish to share this with the people you love, consider the reception you might receive and the overall benefit to the relationship. Never be dishonest, to yourself or anyone else, about what you believe, but don't overshare unless you feel compelled to do so.

You may also encounter societal pressures from friends or coworkers who have their own spiritual rules and guidelines to which they will compare you. You will find that public opinion may work against you as people struggle to compare your new choices to images of TV and literary witches, fairies, evil queens, Pied Pipers, devil worshippers, and people possessed by demons or evil spirits. Again, I caution against a need for oversharing. I am currently employed by a faith-based organization. As you might guess, Wicca is not the faith of their spiritual focus. I have shared the fact that I am Wiccan with my boss and select members of my team, but do not make a habit of oversharing my spiritual preferences within the workplace. When prayers are offered before meetings or events, I simply bow my head and take a moment to speak to the Creator in my own way. The words may be different but the request is usually the same: *Bless our work in service to those who need it most.* That is a prayer I can embrace, not matter whose "God" is called on when they offer it.

You will also find as you research different alternative traditions that some are very structured. If you feel more connected to the Divine through the use of highly ceremonial Magick and enumerated guidelines, then by all means, feel free to pursue that avenue of worship. Some of the founders of Modern Day Wicca, including Buckland, have laid out step-by-step lessons on "How-To" Wicca. The form of Wicca I practice is very eclectic and embraces ideas from several sources. It has also taken on a life of its own when over time we have created new traditions within our circle that are passed on to those that have joined our group. However you proceed, there is no wrong way of doing it. All great journeys start with a single step.

Deity Exercise:

One of the first things we must do when we begin to practice an alternate form of religion is identify how WE perceive "God." I am sure that we all have an image in our mind of what God might look like. Based on your life experiences, you have been fed images of God by your family, society, church, media, and cinema. But what happens if we take a look at God in a different way? As in the movie, *Oh, God!*, what if God were just a little old man that you happened to encounter in the public restroom? After all, God is everywhere! What if, as in the movie, *Dogma*, God turns out to be a woman? Would all misogynists have to fear for their eternal soul?

So what *does* God look like? Close your eyes and try to picture Him/Her in your mind. Note anything that seems remarkable.

- Does the Creator have a form that can be described or is it pure energy?
- Do you see two or more entities that you associate with "God"?
- Does this entity take a more corporeal form in your mind? Does it radiate with an ethereal glow? Is it angelic or earthly? Is it human or does it take on a more shamanistic visage perhaps?
- If this figure is strictly in human form, is the image male or female? Does it have any outstanding characteristics? Does it appear in your mind as any image particular to ancient Old World culture/tradition or ethnicity?
- Are they clothed in white robes or human garb? Are they clothed in animal skins? Or are they clothed at all?

All of these questions may be difficult to answer immediately. You may have to try this exercise more than once in order get a clear image in your mind. You may also find that doing some research on ancient spiritual traditions from around the globe will aid you in forming this image in your mind. Also realize that as you grow, you may have several images in your mind of Gods and Goddesses from different traditions, both past and present. These images are interchangeable and allow us to work on specific goals with a deity/archetype that is representative of that goal.

I personally picked Celtic and Greco/Roman mythology as my springboard for research. I am of western European descent and, as a child in elementary school, I had grown to love the tales of Gods and Goddesses, heroes and heroines, ruling the Heavens, Earth, and Underworld with a firm hand. I especially loved the stories where they came to Earth and intermingled with their human children. In revisiting these myths, I was able to form a clear picture in my mind of what I thought my personal Gods and Goddesses looked like. I was also called to Celtic tradition as I learned about the Wiccan faith. Many of the modern philosophies also began in Western Europe and were based on traditions that came from their ancestors, the Celts and the Druids.

I have since identified many archetypal images that work for me when connecting to the One. Not all are of European decent and they cover an array of time periods including the present. When beginning your own research, you may find that you connect more easily to some of the histories that relate to your ancestry or ethnic background. However, try not to limit yourself to learning about one tradition to the exclusion of others. Keep an open mind and heart and your vision of your personal Gods/Goddesses will come to you. At the end of this book you will find a list of recommended reading to help you seek your own answers to some of these questions. *

Elements of a Ritual

Much like other faiths, the practice of Wicca involves ritual and ceremony. These rituals can differ in nature from celebratory to divinatory in nature, and can encompass prayers, meditations, or magickal workings. In form, they are the act of creating a sacred space in which to recognize and make contact with the Creator. They can be performed anywhere at any time and can involve deeply ceremonial practices or be spur-of-the-moment based on need or desire. They can include magickal tools, selected and anointed to that end, or can simply involve using items from your surroundings that you have selected for that purpose.

Intent

When designing a ritual, the ritual's intent should be the main focus. What is the "reason for the season"? Is your intent to thank the Creator for all the wonderful gifts in your life? Is your intent to ask for intervention on behalf of the Divine to make some new and seemingly impossible thing a reality? Do you have a need for healing of mind, body, or Spirit for yourself or others? Do you wish to connect with the Collective Consciousness to promote peace and planetary unity? Once you answer this question, it will be easier to design a ritual that is tailored to the desired intent.

Location

The next decision is to select a location to hold the ritual. If you are practicing by yourself, as a solo practitioner, or away from your normal group, it may not require much in the way of space. Your apartment or house can be a great spot to connect with the Divine! So can your yard, a local park, or any spot in Nature that calls to you. As a follower of a Nature religion, I would recommend getting outside and connecting with it as much as possible. However, some people are limited in the amount of outdoor space they have available or feel fearful of practicing in a public place under the eyes of random strangers. I have practiced in an apartment, a house, my yard, my friends' houses and yards, my local park, my pagan campground, and a couple National Forests. All of these were special to me because of the connection made, not necessarily the location. Pick the spot that will encourage the least amount of distractions so that you can concentrate on the intent of your ritual and the Divine connection you will be making.

Constructing the Ceremony

The next step is to develop the ritual or ceremony itself. Traditionally, a Wiccan ceremony comprises the following activities:

- Creating sacred space by Casting a Circle
- Cleansing and Anointing
    - the space
    - the altar and tools being used
    - the practitioners (including yourself)
- Calling the Elements (or Quarters)
- Invocation of the God(s) and Goddess(es)
- The Ceremony (magickal working, meditation, or prayers)
- Thanksgiving to the Divine and the Elements
    - For all the blessings in your life
    - For "One Good Thing" that has happened since

you last worshipped (this is particular to all the circles that I hold)

- Prayer Requests
- Closing of the Circle.

This can be followed by Feasting with Cakes and Ale or just cookies and punch, whatever suits your mood and your crowd. Let's take a look at each of these steps in detail.

Creating Sacred Space

Creating sacred space in which to worship is an important part of the act of ritual. It sets the physical, mental, emotional, and spiritual stage for the ceremony or magickal working that is to come. However, before we delve into magick, I believe that the first sacred space that one should create is not one in the physical world, but one that lives within us. In working with the spirit, sometimes we are forced to deal with uncomfortable issues in order to see our path more clearly. These may be obstacles in our everyday lives but they can also be mental or emotional obstacles, feelings and thought patterns that have been engrained in our psyche since childhood. They can come from society, environment, family, or past religious experiences, and sneak in on us when we are open and vulnerable. Almost always, when forming a true and lasting connection with the Creator, we are asked to challenge those thought-forms, breaking free of bonds that we didn't even know existed in order to fully connect with our *inner* deity, and with the Universe as a whole.

Visualization Exercise:

In order to create this internal sacred "safe space" you will be using a technique called creative visualization. Creative visualization is the technical name for picturing something in your mind. When attempting to achieve any goal, a person would picture the idea and its end result in his mind, perhaps then listing the steps that were needed to complete this goal. Below is a simple example.

I want to paint my bedroom a different color. I picture in my mind what I want it to look like when I am done. Then I make a list, mental or physical, of the steps that need to be taken to achieve that goal:

1. Purchase the desired color paint along with rollers, brushes, edge tape, drop cloths, etc...
2. Move furniture away from walls. Take down any pictures from the walls.
3. Place drop cloths on ground.
4. Tape off corners, etc... to prevent paint bleed.
5. Paint room. Allow dry time.
6. Remove tape and drop cloths. Replace pictures and furniture.
7. Stand back and marvel at your new room!

When applying creative visualization to spiritual endeavors, the steps are a little different but follow the same pattern. In this case, we want to create a safe and sacred space in our mind where we can go and find peace and calm, a place where no harm can come to you. This place is your own! No two people have the same sacred personal place because they are as individual as the person who is creating it. To construct this space, we will use creative visualization in combination with meditation. Below are the steps that you need to complete this exercise.

1. Select a time and place where you can sit comfortably for twenty to thirty minutes. During meditation, it is important not to be disturbed in order to maintain focus and optimize results.

2. If you wish, select some instrumental music that you find soothing and play it on low in the background. You can also use a white noise maker, such as the app on your phone, to create this background sound. This helps the mind block out other external noises that may be present and keeps you from feeling like it is "too quiet."

3. Light a scented candle or some incense, nothing too strong or overwhelming!

4. Relax and close your eyes, clearing your mind of any thought that may creep in from your day. Allow all thoughts of responsibilities, work, family, dinner, etc. . . to leave your mind.

5. Take three deep cleansing breaths. Allow the muscles in your body to relax further, releasing the tension and settling into a comfortable state. Continue to concentrate on your breathing until your mind is clear.

6. Imagine yourself glowing with a white light or energy. This is the God Spirit within you aligning with the Creator. Feel the warmth of the glow throughout your physical body as well as your mind and spirit. Allow the light to become you, and you the light, glowing brighter and brighter.

7. When this has happened, push the light out from your

body slowly, allowing it to create a bubble, or pearl, of light that surrounds you. Let the light expand until the bubble has created a spherical "room." The curve of the bubble should extend below the ground or "floor," connecting you with the Mother, and reach into the sky or to the "ceiling," connecting you with the Father. This is your safe space.

8. Now open your mind's eye and look around! What do you see?

a. Is the bubble transparent or solid? Can you see the sky overhead? Maybe an ornate chandelier?

b. What objects are in your space? Note any natural surroundings if the space is outdoors. Note any furnishings, artwork, knickknacks, or decorations that may be there if the space is an actual room.

c. Is there a scent, a sound, a color, or a feeling that stands out in your mind? Allow yourself to experience it.

9. Spend a few minutes just getting to know every inch of your space. Fill it with your imagination and make it what you wish. Walk around it, sit in reflection, or lie down on that super comfy sofa or lounger. The object is to feel safe, secure, and at home in this magickal space.

10. When you feel completely safe and at home, and have had the chance to explore it all you want for now, settle your mind and begin to picture the images around you glowing with the same white light that created them. Allow the light to encompass everything, until you and the glow are one.

11. Slowly pull back the light or energy until you are back in your own body; recognize the sound of your heart-

beat and the rhythm of your breathing. When you feel ready, slowly flex your fingers and toes, then your arms and legs. Lastly, feel your entire body come to life again. Allow yourself to slowly open your eyes and readjust to your physical surroundings. You have completed your first creative visualization meditation.

In order to solidify this experience, you may wish to sketch your safe place if you are handy with a pencil, write about it in poem or verse, or list the items you saw on a piece of paper. You will be going there many times over the course of your magickal life.

Not all individuals find this meditation easy at first. Creative visualization is a learned skill and improves over time and with repetition. If you find that you are having limited success with this exercise, DON'T GIVE UP! Keep at it until you can calm your mind and enter your safe space with almost no effort. Later we will try to leave our safe space and explore what may be in the "outside" world.

Casting a Circle

Casting a Circle is done to physically and psychically draw a ring of protection around you and those with whom you are practicing. It can be as small or large as suits your need. Using any cleansing and purification tools that you have at your disposal (see examples below), "draw" a circle around the area in which you plan to worship or do magickal work. Moving in a clockwise direction (doesil), envision your space not just as a one-dimensional circle that reaches only the area it touches. Imagine it reaching into the sky above you and the ground beneath you. You are creating a 360 degree bubble that encloses your sacred space, a virtual temple to keep the magick in and the mischief out. Generally, three times around the circle should be enough to complete this task. However, if you are just learning and need a few more "spins around the block" to make your space come to life, by all means, take the time. Magick should never be hurried but entered into with patience and care. Below is a list of cleansing and purification tools that are not required but may aid in completing this task.

- Sage or Sweet Grass smoke (has a cleansing effect)
- Water sprinkled on the ground or floor (you can collect rainwater on a full moon night to give this extra power)
- Salt, added to the water or by itself
- A cord or rope (can be used to outline the area)
- The blade or point of an athame, sword, wand, or staff (can be used to draw the circle in the air or on the ground)
- Candles (can be placed around the circle and lit all at once or one at a time as you make your way)—fire safety first!
- Broom (to sweep away unwanted energy)
- Any elements of nature, (i.e., flower pedals, autumn leaves, pine cones, fruits or herbs, etc.,)—strewn around the area you are purifying

Typically, once the space has been created, the construction of an altar, the central hub of the circle, is the next step in the process. Most of the Wiccans I know keep an altar in their house somewhere and change it occasionally to fit the seasons of the year, the needs of the day, or the focus of their current goals. Altars can be as simple or as complex as you desire. They can be traditional in nature or may take on a unique form, and should be representative of the purpose of the ritual or ceremony for which they are being used. This is a holy construction and should be done with your spiritual goals in mind, and with reverence and respect to the Creator and the Elements. However, a touch of whimsy or fun and creativity is also appropriate for your altar.

An altar usually has a centerpiece that represents the Creator, or God and Goddess, you will be praying to. Additionally, the altar traditionally includes items that represent the compass points of the Elements, North, East, South, and West. Candles, flowers, bells, censors, chalices, pentacles, crosses, and ankhs are also found on some altars, and are used to aid in connecting with the subconscious mind and enhancing the various portions of the ceremony.

Altar Exercise:

Using any flat surface, construct an altar.

1. Determine North, East, South, and West. Place an object that represents that Element or direction. Possible objects that may be used for this purpose are listed below.

	North	East	South	West
Season	Winter	Spring	Summer	Fall
Flower	Carnation, Evergreen, Columbine	Lavender, Lilac, Daisy, Iris, Tulip	Sunflower, Marigold, Cock's Cone	Water Lily, Sweet Pea, Rose
Herb/ Spice	Sage, Sweet Grass, Lemongrass	Oregano, Parsley, Basil	Cumin, Cayenne, Cinnamon	Coriander, Dill, Thyme
Animal	Bear, Stag, Buffalo, Horses, Bulls	Birds, Butterflies, Dragonflies	Lizards, Salamanders, Snakes	Dolphins, Whales, Fish, Seahorses
Incense	Patchouli	Frankincense	Amber	Lavender
Tool	Cauldron, Mortar/Pestle, Pentagram	Dagger, Sword, Censor	Candle, Wand/Staff, Flint/Steel	Chalice, Seashell, Crystal
Colors (for candles, altar cloth, etc...)	Green, Brown, Black	White, Yellow, Purple	Orange, Red, Gold	Blue, Pink, Silver
Magickal Creatures	Dryads, Elves, Dwarves	Fairies, Sylphs, Angels	Dragons, Undines, Serpents	Mermaids, Nymphs, Sea Monsters

2. In the center of the altar, place a symbol of the God/Goddess. This could be one object or two, one for each Deity. The item you choose can represent a particular God/Goddess, can represent the archetype of each figure, or can represent a central Divine Creator. Below is a list of items that could be used as your centerpiece:

God	Goddess
Sun Figurine	Moon Figurine
Statue of a Man	Statue of a Woman
Yin Symbol	Yang Symbol
Gold Candle	Silver Candle
Any picture of your chosen God	Any picture of your chosen Goddess

Items you choose that have some personal meaning to you will probably work best.

3. Light any candles or incense that you have on your altar. Allow yourself to be immersed in the scent or light rising from the altar, clearing your mind and focusing on your creation.

4. Meditate on your completed altar. Note how it makes you feel. Remember, there is no right or wrong way to do this. The altar is only an outer symbol of your inner intentions. Feel free to change the construct of your altar at any time. Try interchanging items on your altar with others based on a particular theme, season, or holiday. Then meditate on your new construction and see how it differs in the way it helps you connect to the Elements and the Creator.

Cleansing and Anointing

The act of cleansing and anointing is performed to begin the transformation of mind, body, and Spirit into an open and Magickal creature, ready to receive the Divine gifts of the God and Goddess. It also helps engage your subconscious mind through the senses using imagery, scent, touch, and hearing, and invokes the Elements of Nature. Sage, sweet grass, or the incense of your choice may be used for the act of cleansing. If you are by yourself, you can simply wave the smoking censor or sage stick around your body, being careful not to touch any of the burning material to your skin, hair, or clothing, and speak the words,

With Air and Fire, I am cleansed. So mote it Be.

Allow yourself to pause and breathe in the aroma of the smoke, and begin to shrug off all the things in the outside world that have been bothering you. Forget about work, about the dog or the doctor's appointment, or the final exam that you are studying for, and just be in the moment.

If you are with a group, the Priest and Priestess can perform these tasks. You can also select one or more persons to perform this function for the group. Be sure that they include themselves in this process. Waving the sage stick or censor around the participant from head to toe, front and back, say the words,

With Fire and Air, I cleanse thee. So Mote it Be!

Much as you did with Fire and Air, you will anoint yourself as a tool of the God and Goddess. You may use salt water for this purpose, but you can also use your favorite essential oil, which is made of elements from both Earth and Water. Be careful when selecting oil for your ceremony. Do not pick one that is likely to cause an adverse reaction when applied to the skin. Cinnamon, for instance, is known to burn if too much is used, and some can cause more of an allergic reaction than others. They do make a huge variety of essential oils which are readily available for purchase and can be selected specifically to match the purpose behind the ritual. Using the items of your choice, rub a small amount of the liquid on your forehead at the "third eye" position (just above the eyebrows in the center of the forehead) and say the words,

With Water and Earth, I am anointed. So Mote it Be.

Or, in the case of a group setting,

With Water and Earth, I anoint thee. So Mote it Be.

While the typical Wiccan uses the sign of a Pentagram to make this mark on the forehead, it is not required to be effective and may be switched to any symbol of your choice, including a cross. This will complete the process and ready the person to move forward with the ceremony. It is appropriate to walk the circumference of the circle, acknowledging the various Elements and the Creator as you do so and clearing your mind of any outside thoughts while in the sacred circle.

Calling the Quarters

We call upon the elements to link ourselves to the Universe and to awaken their energies within us. Each element represents not only the natural world but also an aspect of ourselves as creatures of nature. By invoking them, we connect ourselves to all the tools that the Gods have given us and commit 100 percent of our energy to the goals we are trying to accomplish.

Earth

For millennia, the human species concentrated on survival alone as its most basic concern. The Paleolithic Era, the Stone Age, and the Iron Age all passed during the development of mankind as a physical being. In nature, it is represented by the planet itself and by all things that grow in the ground and live on the land. Trees, plants, creatures of the forest and the field, caves and canyons are all symbols of Earth. Its season is winter and its time of day midnight until just before dawn. In human beings, this element is represented by our physical body and its struggle to survive. Hunting, growing crops, baking and harvesting, building shelters, and keeping the body protected from the heat and cold are all part of this element. It is the home and hearth, the stability of a good job, and being physically healthy and active. It also represents the womb from which we all come and to which we all return. In this way, Earth is considered a feminine or passive element.

As with all things in existence, where there are positive aspects there are also negative ones. The long harsh winter, frostbite, earthquakes, and cave-ins are associated with this element. Homelessness, job problems, starvation, and maladies that deal with the body such as cancer, gastrointestinal distress, athlete's foot, and dental concerns are all based in Earth. If we are trying to banish disease from our body, or poor eating or spending habits from our routine, we should consider working with the tools of Earth. Remember that *we* are the greatest tool that we have at our disposal. Our body, as a tool of Earth, is a temple unto itself, housing our precious soul, the part that is God energy in its purest form. Always treat it with respect for without it, there is no human existence.

Below is an example of a basic invocation to Earth:

> *We call upon the Spirit of Earth,*
> *That which dwells in the fields and forests,*
> *Which lives in the caves and grottos,*
> *And is our home and our hearth,*
> *Come to us.*
> *Strengthen our bodies and allow us to sustain ourselves in times of plenty and sallow.*
> *Fill our tables with bounty, and bestow upon us stability and good fortune.*
> *As I will, so mote it be.*

Water

After mankind figured out how to survive on a strictly physical level, he began to concentrate on concerns of the emotions and the heart. The Dark Ages and the Renaissance Era both came to pass during the emotional development of mankind. In nature, Water is represented by rain and rainbows, creeks and streams, rivers and lakes, the ocean, and the Moon. All creatures that dwell within the waters are also part of this realm. In human beings, this aspect is represented by our emotions and the choices we make that are ruled by them. Romantic love, friendship, compassion, sympathy and empathy, and gentle healing and cleansing are all part of this element. It is the feeling of love for your family and friends, the romance you feel with your partner when you cuddle and kiss, and the desire to treat others with kindness. It is also the way we express ourselves through painting and sculpting, music and dancing, poetry and storytelling, and all forms of artistic endeavor. Because the tides are controlled by the Moon and relate to a woman's menstrual flow, Water is also considered a feminine or passive element.

Water is also the element of tidal waves, monsoons, floods, and raging storms. It produces fear, anger, jealousy, resentment, and betrayal in its negative form. It also rules depression and broken-heartedness. Maladies of the circulatory system such as anemia, low or high blood sugar, diabetes, and high blood pressure, palpitations, and arrhythmias are also associated with this element. If we are trying to control the above ailments, heal ourselves of loss, sadness, loneliness, or rejection, or if we want to build lasting friendships or find a true love, we should consider working with this element.

As a practitioner, artistic expression and religious ceremony are ways of connecting with your heart. All endeavors of this nature tie the conscious mind, which concentrates on "matters at hand" to the subconscious, which recognizes the symbolism expressed by creations of beauty and reverence. In this way, we are accessing the 90 percent of our brain that generally lies in the background, the subconscious, while we go about our business using only 10 percent of our mind for conscious thought. Imagine the potential of mankind when we focus all 100 percent of its power to direct our thoughts and actions! With intent, we can direct this power toward our goals and our spiritual growth.

Below is an example of a basic invocation to Water:

We call upon the Spirit of Water,
That which dwells in the rivers and streams,
Which lives in the lakes and oceans,
And is our heart and healing power.
Come to us.
Cleanse us and allow us to share happiness and friendship.
Fills us with love and compassion, and bestow upon us peace and contentment.
As I will, so mote it be!

Air

When, as a species, we came to recognize ourselves as creatures of emotion, we began to think of ways that we could direct both our survival skills and our self-expression in more logical and practical ways. This stage of human development has come to be referred to as the Industrial Age. In nature, Air is represented by birds and butterflies, clouds and mountain peaks, breezes and gale force winds. In human beings, Air is mental clarity, forethought, insight, logic, and psychic ability. It inspires us to invent and intuit, trying to anticipate the future and our needs as a people, combining our knowledge of metals, textiles, agriculture and healing to create devices that could improve our quality of life. We invent machinery, advance in communication and medicinal techniques, and discover new ways to travel, even reaching the moon and shooting toward the stars. Because invention and logic are aggressive endeavors, Air is considered a male element.

On the negative side, Air is also the element of tornadoes, and manifests itself in the human experience as confusion, scattering the thought patterns and creating a cloud of second-guessing and doubt. It is also the element of mental illness and psychosis. If we want to work on clearing the mind, gaining insight into an unclear situation, or breaking obsessive compulsive behaviors, we should concentrate our efforts on this element.

As a practitioner of magick, thoughts and ideas can be tangible, like how to balance a checkbook, or they can be intangible. Dreams, intuition, psychic abilities, and astral projection are all forms of intangible thought-forms. This is another path that the mind uses to connect us with the Universe and all the knowledge within it. Meditation, trance work, dream interpretation, scrying with a crystal ball or mirror, or using divinatory tools, such as tarot cards, runes, or tea leaves, are all ways of unlocking the mind. If we learn to study and interpret these messages, we will become more in tune with the Collective Consciousness, that piece of ourselves that is linked to the past and the future, to all of mankind and to the Creator. We can simultaneously harness the knowledge of the Ancients who have gone before us and use forethought and insight to direct our actions in a positive and meaningful way for the benefit of man and the planet.

Below is a basic invocation to Air:

We call upon the Spirit of Air,
That which dwells in the clouds and high mountain peaks,
Which flits on the breeze and soars the clear blue sky,
And is our intellect and intuition.
Come to us!
Clear our minds of confusion and allow us to see that which is not apparent.
Fill us with inspiration and insight, and bestow upon us wisdom.
As I will, so mote it be!

Fire

With physical survival part of our routine, and using our emotions to create beauty, happiness, and joy, we have embraced the thought that success alone is not enough. We recognize that we are not islands unto ourselves but part of a greater mystery. This is the mystery of our creation and our purpose in the Universe. For some, this stage of human development is known as the Age of Aquarius. In nature, the power of Fire to create and destroy is represented by the Big Bang Theory, the explosion that created the Universe and us as its children. It is lightning, striking and causing the forest fire that can propagate the seeds to sow a new crop of trees. It is the forge, through which all materials are changed and formed with heat and hammer. In human beings, it rules unbridled lust and is the soul of passion, that which makes us seek procreation of the species, to bring to life new versions of ourselves, just as the Gods did when creating us. It is the desire to make from raw materials something that is new and different, one of a kind. It is also the yearning to seek our Creator and know our source, to bond with all mankind and save ourselves from our own destructive nature. Because creation and destruction are both aggressive, Fire is viewed as a masculine element.

Fire is a raging inferno, scorching everything in its path, leaving nothing behind. It is also the element of war, the clash of the sword and the quest for power and domination. If we allow Fire to rule our lives or our planet, we will be destined to war within ourselves and with each other. However, if we want to create a new beginning, viewpoint, or attitude, purge bad thoughts or actions from our lives, banish strong negativity or destructive thought-forms, and forge a lasting peace in our soul and on our planet, we would want to work with this element.

As a practitioner of magick, Fire is the call to recognize humanity as creatures of the Divine Spirit and to harness that spirit to make change, to transform our way of life and foster peace and global harmony. Flame gazing is a particularly good method of receiving messages and creative ideas from the Universe. Writing a thought, idea, or need onto a piece of parchment and then burning it, allowing the smoke to carry your message to the Gods, is also a method of working with Fire. For banishing bad habits, such as smoking or overeating, try burning a cigarette (not with your lips, ha ha) or the label from your favorite package of junk food. But remember that fire can be all-consuming. It must be handled with care, respected at all times, and sought with correct intent so as not to get burned in the process.

Below is a basic invocation to Fire:

> *We call upon the Spirit of Fire,*
> *That which dwells in the arid deserts and volcanic ash,*
> *Which lives in the forges and warms our core,*
> *And is our passion and creation.*
> *Come to us!*
> *Light within us the spark of creation and allow us to create and procreate,*
> *Fill us with passion and give us the desire to seek out our soul.*
> *As I will, so mote it be!*

While I have discussed above the development of mankind as a species in very general terms, I feel it important to note that at no time in history have any of the elements existed without the others. During our survival stage (Earth), we documented our experiences as works of art on cave walls (Water), invented the wheel (Air), and discovered fire (Fire, obviously). During the Dark Ages and Renaissance Period (Water), we established territorial boundaries (Earth), developed reading, writing, and mathematics (Air), and waged Holy Wars (Fire). During our industrial period (Air), we have modernized our basic existence with conveniences (Earth), leaving more time for development of lasting and meaningful relationships with family and friends (Water), and reached beyond ourselves globally and extra-terrestrially, to discover more about ourselves as a race and as creatures of a greater universe (Fire).

Thus, as we begin our Spiritual Age (Fire), we are finding ways to combat the damage that we have done to our planet due to global warming and overpopulation (Earth), recognizing that emotionally we all feel, want, need the same sense of love and compassion and happiness as any other of our species (Water), and we are harnessing the technology at our disposal to link ourselves together in a way that has never before been known by man (Air). We have only to discover that part of ourselves that is the Divine Spirit, to go beyond our own existence and link ourselves together as one Collective Consciousness so that we may be as one with each other, the Earth, and the Universe. Easier said than done, right?

If we have identified ourselves as spiritual creatures and begun the journey to enlightenment, we are already on the path to the highest level of human experience. However, being a spiritual person is not just a moment of reverence or ritual, not just the deeds you have done in the name of some God or another; it is in the living of everyday life with an awareness of the effect that we have on each living creature we touch that makes us a spiritual being. In all our actions, thoughts, and discoveries, we should be striving to act in a way that is loving and generous, that nurtures Nature and all its creations, and preserves human dignity and growth. Bringing spirituality into our daily existence is the surest way to keep our feet on the path to enlightenment.

Invocation of the God and Goddess

You may have noticed that the above Calling the Quarters only used four of the five elements that I discussed earlier in this book. That's because when I call the fifth Element, I am calling on the inner God and Goddess *as* I call to the Divine Spirit of the God and Goddess. Thus, the Invocation is simultaneously calling the fifth Element and the Divine Creator. This is the final step in linking all the elements of the conscious and subconscious to a single purpose. It is also recognition of the fact that we are only a part of that which is All, the Alpha and the Omega, the Beginning and the End of all things in the Universe. By invoking the Divine, we *become* the Divine, capable of performing miracles and answering prayers by being integrally linked with Divine Energy.

The Goddess

Over the years, I have read many texts on the subject of religions and traditions and was amazed when I discovered remnants of the Goddess all but hidden within the Holy Bible. So much effort had gone into the demonization of women during the development of the Christian faith that I am surprised this text wasn't muddled beyond understanding. And yet, as we read from the pages of Proverbs 8, we can hear the voice of the Goddess Sophia, Wisdom, the Holy Spirit, speak to Her worshippers.

Does not Wisdom call out? Does not understanding raise Her voice?

On the heights along the way, where the paths meet, She takes Her stand;

Beside the gates leading into the city, at the entrances, she cries aloud:

"To you, O men, I call out; I raise My voice to all mankind. You who are simple, gain prudence; you who are foolish, gain understanding. Listen, for I have worthy things to say; I open My lips to speak what is right. My mouth speaks what is true, for My lips detest wickedness. All the words of My mouth are just; none of them is crooked or perverse. To the discerning all of them are right; they are faultless to those who have knowledge. Choose My instruction instead of silver, knowledge rather than choice gold, for wisdom is more precious than rubies, and nothing you desire can compare with Her.

"I, Wisdom, dwell together with prudence; I possess knowledge and discretion. ... Counsel and sound judgment are mine; I have understanding and power...I love all those who love Me, and those who seek to find Me. With me are riches and honor, bestowing wealth on those who love me and making their treasures full. The Lord possessed me at the beginning of His work, before His deeds of old; I

*was appointed from eternity, from the beginning, before the world began. When there were no oceans, I was given birth, when there were no springs abounding with water; before the mountains were settled in place, before the hills, I was given birth, before He made the Earth or its fields or any of the dust of the world. I was there when He set the Heavens in place, when he marked out the horizon on the face of the deep, when He established the clouds above and fixed securely the fountains of the deep, when He gave the sea its boundary so the waters would not overstep His command, and when He marked the foundations of the Earth. Then I was the craftsman at His side. I was filled with delight day after day, rejoicing always in His presence, rejoicing in His whole world and delighting in mankind."*3

As the patriarchal Christian church was formed and doctrine established, statues and temples dedicated to Sophia were not in line with the message of the One God. Therefore, the Goddess Sophia was canonized by the Catholic Church as St. Sophia, reduced to one of the four Charities: St. Faith, St. Hope, St. Charity, and St. Sophia (Wisdom). Her importance and power was stripped from Her and today, She is hardly known. However, this passage from the Old Testament suggests that the Goddess has been around since before the One God.

The Goddess, or Lady, of the Wiccan faith can be worshipped as one central figure but is also known to have three aspects: Maiden, Mother, and Crone. As the Maiden, she is the flowers that spring forth from the soil in springtime, the forest nymph that calls your inner lust to the fore. She is embodied by the young lady from infancy to adolescence, and is lovely and passionate, innocent, and coming into the realization of Her own fertility. She is the promise of life to come. As the Mother,

---

3 4 New York International Bible Society;1978/ The Holy Bible – NIV Version – pg. 686-687./ International Bible Society.

She is the Earth, fertile and luscious. She brings us forth into the physical realm and holds and nurtures us as we grow to be adults and parents. She is the love and passion of womanhood, the protector of children, the healer of the sick, and the Nurturer. She holds us in her embrace as we discover the mysteries of the Universe and ourselves. As the Crone, She is the grandmother, the teacher, and the comforter. She lends us her wisdom and leads us through the dark to the other side of life with strength, humility, and grace. In totality, She is the source from which we come and to which we will return. She is Gaia, Mother Earth!

She is also known as the Moon, which is the celestial and mysterious representation of Her many aspects. By invoking Her, we ask for all these qualities to be present in our ceremonies and our lives.

Here is an example of a Basic Invocation to the Goddess:

I call upon the Goddess, Maiden, Mother and Crone,
She who is the Moon in the Heavens,
Shine from beyond the veil and be present here in this circle.
Open our eyes so that we may see what cannot be seen,
Open our ears so that we may hear what cannot be heard,
And Open our minds so that we may know the Unknowable.
Be here now! So Mote it Be!

The God

With the exception of those raised as a hereditary witch or those who were raised in Native American or other tribal or ancient traditions, most readers will find that they are (or have been) hereditary practitioners of a patriarchal religion. I, for one, was raised in the Christian faith. This faith puts forth the concept that there is one God, or perhaps a trinity of Spirits that make up one God, categorized as the Father, the Son, and the Holy Spirit. All of these figures are decidedly male. Along with the Christians, worshippers of the Jewish traditions, as well as adherents to the Islamic faith and Buddhism, have been taught to worship a central male figure known as God, Jehovah, Allah, JHWH (pronounced yah-way), Jesus, or Buddha. As a result, you probably already have an image of God in your mind that is based on your prior learning or tradition. While I would not encourage you to desert your traditional teachings on a whim, I do want to encourage you to re-examine the image of God that has been placed in your mind by heredity or society. You have the freedom to redefine and develop your own image of who God is to you, one that best fits the person you are as a new spiritual being.

The God, or Lord, of the Wiccan faith is as complex as his counterpart. He can also be worshipped as one central figure but has three aspects: the Acolyte, the Hunter, and the Sage. As the Acolyte, he plays in the fields, embracing curiosity and imagination to discover what is new. He explores the boundaries of his world with fearlessness and an insatiable desire. He represents life from infancy to adolescence as well, and experiences lust, pride, and protectiveness. He begins to seek She who is His other half. As the Hunter, He is the Stag, running through the forest with purpose and prowess. He stands beside us as we work and play, while supporting ourselves, our family, and our community. He keeps us lean, keeps our "eyes on the prize," and *is* the definition of adaptability, ingenuity, and prowess. He is the Provider and is with us when we need strength and courage. As the Sage, He is old, weathered, and wise beyond our grasp. He has seen all, done all, and still represents joy and peace of Spirit. Having lived a full life of wonder, He readily submits Himself to the sacrifice that is the Turning of the Wheel for He knows without doubt that He will be born again. As a celestial body, He is the Sun. Radiant, awesome, and powerful, He is always there even if we can't see him, reflected by the Goddess in the night sky.

Here is a basic invocation to the God:

> *I call upon the God, Acolyte, Hunter, Sage,*
> *He who is the Sun in the Sky.*
> *Shine down your Light and be present in our circle.*
> *Open our eyes to that which is clearly seen,*
> *Open our ears to that which is clearly heard,*
> *And Open our minds to that which is logical and sensible.*
> *Be here now! So Mote it Be!*

Note that you may call on any or all of these aspects when performing a ritual, and may wish to call only one aspect if you are dealing with a problem or desire that is strictly male or female in origin, such as menstruation or low testosterone. When designing your invocations, whether to the Elements or the God and Goddess, feel free to tailor them to the goal of the ceremony, the season of the year, or the life event that you are commemorating.

Now that all of the cast members are in play, the main body of the ritual can be addressed. What is it that you are trying to accomplish? This is where you address that specifically. Whatever your goal, spell it out in no uncertain terms. The Divine works best when it has clear, positive requests to focus on. If you want a new job, ask for one. If you want to lose weight, or quit smoking, or form better relationships with your family, ask for that! Place faith in the fact that anything can come to pass! Manifestation of the spoken word is a real tool in making things happen. Also, don't give in to the notion that you don't deserve whatever it is you need. The Gods are generous and loving and wants us all to be healthy and happy! But They also need our help. So, make it a point of doing your part to keep yourself pointed in the right direction. Be open for signs that may lead you to opportunities, and take what is offered with gratitude, knowing that all things happen for a reason. If the Gods are trying to show you the way, and your eyes are closed, they may have a tough time leading you down the path to enlightenment.

Beltane is the Wiccan celebration of the Union of the God and the Goddess. This union is recognized as that which created the Universe and everything in existence. On Beltane, 2002, we performed this ritual as part of a Celebration of the Masculine and the Feminine. It contains all the previously covered invocations and a Magickal working, which involves creating some new aspect of our lives as individuals. Oddly, a group is a great place to get individual work done. It affords you the energy of many worshippers focused on your individual goals or desires.

A Beltane Ritual

An Altar was set up with a maypole nearby for dancing. Ribbons, each in a color chosen by the participant, were attached to the Pole before it was erected. Quarter candles, a red Center Candle, and Flowers were all placed on the altar along with any personal items the attendees wished to add to it. Then we created a sacred space by smudging and sprinkling the area with saltwater, walking the perimeter to establish a magickal bubble in which to worship. Then we cleansed and anointed all participants.

Quarters

I call upon the Sylphs, the fairies of the Wind, to fly forth from your treetops and mountain peaks. Clear our minds and open our third eye to new thoughts and ideas. In love, we welcome you to our circle, oh, Spirits of the East! So Mote it be!

I call upon the Undines, the fairies of the Water, to swim forth from your crystal fountains and foaming oceans. Wash away our woes and heal our hearts with tender grace.

In love, we welcome you to our circle, oh, Spirits of the West. So Mote it be!

I call upon the Salamanders, fairies of Fire, to erupt forth from your volcanoes and bonfires. Forge our Spirits and form our desires into sizzling lava. In love, we welcome you to our circle, oh, Spirits of the South. So Mote it be!

I call upon the Gnomes, fairies of the Earth, to venture forth from your cool dark caves and thick old forests. Let us stand on solid ground as the Mother springs forth with all Her bounty. In love, we welcome you to our circle, oh, Spirits of the North. So Mote it be!

As we called to each direction, we would face that way, addressing and inviting the Spirit of the Element to join us in the circle.

Invocation

I call upon the Goddess, Flora, Queen of the May, dance into our presence as the flowers ever blooming in the sun.

Representative of the Goddess, usually a newly initiated female member of group, dances forth from the group of participants.

With Your radiance, You bring forth your Consort.

Strong young male initiate begins to stir and step forward, attracted to Her.

Sensing you, needing you, he would defeat any that stand in his way.

As he begins to "stalk" her, the High Priest stands in his way, challenging him with staff. A mock battle ensues and the young buck is victorious, winning His place beside Her.

For now is the time of the Mating, the union of that which is opposite and yet the same.

The "God and Goddess" embrace.

As we welcome you, we welcome the God at Your side.

The "God and Goddess" step forward, taking from the Priestess the dagger and chalice. A symbolic version of the Great Rite is performed in the circle with the Priest inserting the dagger into the Chalice held by the Maiden.

May You bless us and become us on this Beltane day!

Ceremony

Since the beginning, creatures of the God and Goddess have brought forth new life onto this planet. We as humans have only recently, in the grand scheme of things, come to the knowledge that is procreation. Yet the life cycle is so deeply engrained in our primal being that we have followed these urges throughout all time.

As mankind struggled for answers to the meaning of life and our place and purpose in the Universe, women were revered as the source of all life because they could produce new life. Goddess religions began to form and we as a race continued to grow.

Then the pendulum swung in the opposite direction. The

male counterpart demanded recognition and power and the mysteries of childbirth and reproduction were deduced through logic and reasoning. God worship became the dominant world focus and children took their father's names.

Today we are beginning a new stage of existence. We as a family of humanity are becoming more aware than ever that men and women are actually equal, although different in many ways. The concepts of old religions, both matriarchal and patriarchal, were valid as spiritual tools for those who believed in them, and are also adaptable to those who seek to believe now. As we grow, as individuals and as a group, let us recognize the importance of an all-encompassing worship of the Divine. Let us embrace our brothers and sisters in the creation of a religious space where all can be free to recognize their Creator in infinitesimal ways. So Mote it Be!

A hug can be passed clockwise around the circle at this point.

Let us now take a moment to meditate on creation. Creation takes on many forms. Every day we create opportunities, friendships, partnerships, marriages, feelings, thoughts, and realities. I want you to think about what you would create in your life. In a moment, as a circle, we will chant these words:

Without woman, there can be no man. Without man, there can be no woman.

Repeat the chant at least three times.

As I come forward with the chalice, the athame shall be passed from person to person. When it reaches you, dip the blade into the chalice three times and announce to the group and the Spirits that which you would create for yourself. May the Lord and Lady of the May bring these things into reality as Their Union brought forth the Universe. So Mote it be!

The blade and chalice were passed around the circle. As each participant stated their intention, the group chanted the worshipper's word(s) to bring magickal energy to that request. Once the entire circle has participated, energy from the chant should be sent into the Heavens. After it has been spent, grounding will be necessary. Encourage members to place their hands on the floor or ground and allow the leftover energy to ebb from them into the Earth.

This is the ceremony as I wrote it all those years ago. Often I made notes so that I, or others who were in my circle, would be able to reproduce the ritual if they wished.

Closing the Circle

When closing a circle, it is always important to ground any excess energy that has been built through the course of the working. Otherwise the participants are likely to feel a bit confused or lightheaded. This feeling will pass as the energy level in your body returns to normal and the subconscious portals you have opened begin to close again. That is why we perform another call to the Spirits, thanking them for their presence and attention, and bidding them farewell.

The call goes something like this:

God and Goddess, Great All and Nothing, thank you for your presence in this circle. Thank you for answering our prayers, for hearing our songs, for feeling our hearts, and for all that you have given us! May you go but never leave us!

So Mote it Be!

To the Element of Air, thank you for your presence in this circle. Thank you for new thoughts and insight, for inspiration, dreams, and seeing beyond the horizon. May you go but never leave us. So Mote it Be!

To the Element of Fire, thank you for your presence in this circle. Thank you for lighting a fire inside me, and giving me the passion and courage to create something new and exciting. May you go but never leave us. So Mote it Be!

To the Element of Water, thank you for your presence in this circle. Thank you for love in our lives, for friendship, and for healing of heart, mind, and body. May you go but never leave us. So Mote it Be!

To the Element of Earth, thank you for your presence in this circle. Thank you for home, health, work, family, and stability. May you go but never leave us. So Mote it Be!

The circle is now closed. Merry meet, merry part, and merry meet again! Blessed Be!

Usually we take the opportunity to feast, potluck, barbecue, or have light appetizers or treats. It allows us to get our bodies and minds back onto the physical plane plus it is always great to commune with your brothers and sisters after the ritual is completed. It also gives you the opportunity to compare experiences you may have had during meditations, etc.

Ritual Exercise

Time to get down to business! Let's start out with a generic ritual to practice your newfound knowledge. Celebrating a holiday or life event is a great reason to hold a ritual but expressing gratitude also presents an excellent opportunity to connect with the Divine. Taking the time to live in the present and to recognize all the positive people and things in your life is amazingly rejuvenating and great for your personal sanity. Honoring and giving thanks to the Source of inspiration, creativity, love, and stability is one way of reminding ourselves to stay in the moment.

For this exercise, you will need to find a space where you can easily set up an altar and create a sacred space without being disturbed. If you have done the previous altar exercise, you should be able to accomplish this part with some amount of ease. Items you may need include, but are not limited to:

- A flat surface on which to form your altar: a blanket on the ground or floor, a tree stump or large rock, a table or mantel.
- A representation of each of the four Elements: choose items you have used earlier or select others from your home or natural surroundings.
- A representation of the God/Goddess: this can be one or multiple items.
- A smudge stick or incense and essential oil or water with a bit of salt in it for the cleansing and anointing.
- A compass (in case you need help determining the directions of the Elements).
- A lighter for any candles or incense you may have. Also, some water in case you need to extinguish the flames from any of those items quickly.
- Any other items that are personal or special to you in some way. Be as creative, decorative, or expressive as you wish.

Once you have gathered these items together, construct your altar and ready yourself to begin.

1. Facing North at the South end of the altar, close your eyes and stand quietly, clearing your mind of all thoughts. Breathe deeply, in and out, focusing on your breath as you clear your mind. When you are free of all thoughts, open your eyes and begin the ritual.

2. Light the smudge/incense and walk it around your altar three times. Three is a magical number and repetition helps seal intent. In the case of a mantel altar, smudge the mantel in an arch extending from each corner of the mantel while picturing the circle extending through the wall and back, completing the circle. Say the words,

With Fire and Air, I cleanse this space.

Place the smudge stick/incense in a fire-safe container on the altar.

3. Pick up the essential oil or salt water. Walking around the altar thrice more, sprinkle oil/salt water with your fingertips and say the words,

With Water and Earth, I anoint this space.

Replace the oil/water on the altar.

4. Facing East, lift your hands, palms up, so that they are in front of you and close your eyes. You may also walk around the altar until you are standing in the eastern quadrant of the circle. Take a deep breath and say the

following (or feel free to create your own invocations):

I call upon the direction of East, Spirit of Air. As I gather to give thanks, come into my circle. Lend me your inspiration, your insight, your wisdom, and make my Spirit light as a feather. So mote it be!

5. Face/walk to the direction of South. Lift your hands, palms up, and close your eyes. Take a deep breath and say the following:

I call upon the direction of South, Spirit of Fire. As I gather to give thanks, come into my circle. Lend me your creativity, your passion, your energy, and forge my Spirit like a sword on the anvil. So mote it be!

6. Face or walk to the West. Lift your hands, palms up, and close your eyes. Take a deep breath and say the following:

I call upon the direction of West, Spirit of Water. As I gather to give thanks, come into my circle. Lend me your healing, your compassion, your love, and fill my Spirit with waves of gratitude. So mote it be!

7. Face or walk to the North. Lift your hands, palms up, and close your eyes. Take a deep breath and say the following:

I call upon the direction of North, Spirit of Earth. As I gather to give thanks, come into my circle. Lend me your stability, your nurturing, your prosperity, and renew my Spirit after the long night. So mote it be!

8. Resume your position on the South side of the altar. While facing it, close your eyes, raise your palms upward, and say the following:

I call upon the Creator, the Divine Spirit, the Mother and Father, Yin and Yang, Within and Without! As I gather to give thanks, come into my circle! Fill me with gratitude for the many gifts that you have bestowed on me. Fill me with humility that I play but a small part in the Great Mysteries of the Universe. Fill me with awe of your boundless love and fullness. Make my Spirit soar that **I am You**, *Who are Pure Energy and Timeless Infinity! So mote it be!*

Alternately, you may also call the God and Goddess individually.

9. Spend a few moments making a mental list of all of the things in your life for which you are thankful. Picture them as clearly as you can and "send" those images to the Creator and into the Universe. Life presents many opportunities to be appreciative if we take the time to stop and recognize them. You may also state them out loud to the Gods and the Universe.

    Some possibilities for which to be thankful:

    a. Family and friends, your children, your pets, your lover

    b. Physical health or recovery from an illness or injury

    c. A home, prosperity, stability, a job or recent promotion

    d. Hobbies or avocations that make your life more

enjoyable

10. After a few moments, clear your mind of any images that have formed and begin to return to your ceremony. Some worshippers will leave a small token of gratitude behind, a sacrifice. This can be something small like a stone, a leaf, nuts, berries, or flowers, on or in the ground near where there altar is placed. Others may burn a hand-drawn or written note that represents what they are thankful for. Some seasoned practitioners will leave a token on their permanent altars which, in themselves, are living and evolving things. Note that this is not necessary and that a truly positive and mentally healthy adherent of any faith does not sacrifice any living thing, in whole or in part, to signify their connection to the Divine.

11. Thank the Creator(s) for their presence in the circle. They have "a lot going on" and you want to seal the deal with more thankfulness. Once again, close your eyes, raise your palms, and say the following:

Divine Mother, Holy Father, Creator of the Universe and all that dwells within, thank you for joining me in this sacred place. Thank you for hearing my prayer, for knowing my heart, and for all of my many blessings. May you go but never leave me! So mote it be!

If you have a candle(s) representing the God/Goddess, extinguish them at this time.

12. While facing the East, say the following:

Direction of East, Spirit of Air, thank you for your presence in my circle. May your inspiration, intuition, and second sight be my companions. May you go but never leave me. So mote it be!

13. Face the South and say the following:

Direction of South, Spirit of Fire, thank you for your presence in my circle. May your creativity, passion, and energy be my companions. May you go but never leave me. So mote it be!

14. While facing the West, say the following:

Direction of West, Spirit of Water, thank you for your presence in my circle. May your healing, your compassion, and your love be my companions. May you go but never leave me. So mote it be!

15. Face the North and say the following:

Direction of North, Spirit of Earth, thank you for your presence in my circle. May your stability, your prosperity, and your comfort be my companions. May you go but never leave me. So mote it be!

16. Proceed to the South side of the altar and walk "out" of the circle. If you like, you can use your very own "magick wand," also known as your index finger, to draw an imaginary "door" in the space and "open" it before you exit.

If you are by yourself, treat yourself to your favorite tea or sugary sweet, whatever makes you feel celebratory and a little self-indulgent. If not, enjoy some snacks or a cool beverage with your cohorts. You have just had a meeting with the Divine and it is worthy of a good high five!

Life Stages & Celebrations - The Wheel of the Year

Wiccans follow a spiritual calendar formed around the Wheel of the Year that is considered one cycle of birth, death, and rebirth. On the Wheel of the Year there are eight holidays (holy days), or Sabbats. These are divided into four major and four minor holidays.

As Wiccans follow the Wheel of the Year, we recognize these holidays as celebrations not only to thank the God and Goddess for the myriad of gifts that are showered upon us throughout our lives but also to reinforce the different aspects of our existence as human beings. We are born (Yule), grow from infancy into childhood (Candelmas), enter adolescence and transform into adults (Oestara), marry and/or mate, often procreating as a result (Beltane), and come into the height of our productivity, realizing our individual power (Litha). As we begin to feel the signs of aging, we relish in the accomplishments of the seeds we have sewn (Lughnasaad), and we give thanks, with wisdom, for all the gifts that God(s) has given us (Mabon), until we lay our head down for the last time and pass from the physical world into the realm of spirit (Samhain). Then comes the rebirth, when as pure spirit, we are one with the Divine, we *are* the Divine, and have perfect understanding and enlightenment. We travel to the Summerland where perfect peace and love are ever-present. This is where our next life can be decided, our next mission on this planet determined, and with perfect love and connectivity to all spirits that dwell within and without, our reincarnation can be set into motion. And so the circle begins again as we are reborn in corporeal form to this world and once more become part of the Collective Consciousness (Yule).

Many of the ceremonies I will share are ones I developed when I was High Priestess of the Circle of Friends and subsequently, the Temple of the Lord and Lady. Others were performed when I was a Priestess in a group called The Coven of the Misty Vale. They are based on common themes observed in Wicca but have their own unique twists. Some of these rituals became traditions for our groups and have been followed since the time they were first used.

Yule

Winter Solstice—Minor—the longest night of the year—is between December 19th and 21st, based on planetary positioning. It is a celebration of the birth (rebirth) of the Sun. This is the time of year that we celebrate new life and creation as a whole. Typical ceremonies might include the reading of a Creation myth or the blessing of any new babies born to the members of the group.

As you have probably noticed, all stories have a beginning, middle, and end. The story of Christianity, the Holy Bible, begins with the following words:

In the beginning, God created the Heavens and the Earth...

We may never know how we came to be on this rare and beautiful planet, Earth. This, then, is where creation mythos comes into play. Arguably, the story of the existence of mankind is the most interesting story of all. Theologians, scientists, shamans, and historians have sought this information perhaps since the beginning of human awareness. From the time of the caveman to the present, we have documented our journey on this planet. We first documented the human experience through cave art, drawing on the walls the various acts that mankind performed, from hunting and planting, to wars, to famines and disasters and to birth, death, and rebirth or ascension into Heaven. Then we scribbled this story on papyrus, on tree bark, on pottery, in paintings, in songs and oral tales that passed from one bard to another, and finally, with the written word, in languages that were as varied as the peoples of the world. Now, in the computer age, we have the ability to store, compare, and contrast these stories, looking for common historical accounts and themes that were shared throughout our journey on this planet.

We created mythos to explain how we got here and what we're doing here, and we studied, and continue to study, the Universe and all its creatures to try to define the human condition in terms greater than our logical mind can comprehend. The myriad of experiences and traditions, along with the lack of global communication, allowed each clan, tribe, or culture to create its own tale of creation, with all of the corresponding legends to accompany it. Most were based on the events that shaped the lives of the peoples. The tales of Gods and Goddesses and the creation of mankind were depicted in art forms and shared orally with the people that belonged to a particular tribe or lived in a particular region.

The experts in these tales, the shamans, the priests(esses), often held positions of respect and authority, giving them the power, real or perceived, to make rules and laws, and to speak on behalf of the Creator(s) in answering questions large and small. Some even claimed to channel the Spirits of the Ancestors or to be in direct contact with God, speaking on his (her) behalf on matters of all import. They would perform feats of "magick" or "healing" to impress onlookers with their supernatural abilities. Often they were perceived as powerful or holy simply because they possessed some knowledge of herbalism or the ability to perform illusions that defied the explanation of the people at large. This gave those with the highest charisma, strength, intellect, or passion for a cause the power to gain followers, establish a militia or army, and be in control of the thoughts and actions of mass amounts of people.

This type of power created a religious political hierarchy, or theocracy, in many places around the globe, and a framework for abuse of the masses. Often in history, we see that the fall of a civilization came when the people who were the victims of such abuse rose up and took back the power that was their own, striking down the theological/political system that had arisen through the fanaticism of a power-drunk few with Godlike stature.

Throughout history we have seen many a holy war waged in the name of God(s). The spreading of Christianity around Europe, the Middle East, and Africa is widely known as one of the bloodiest times in history, with armed forces taking over towns, villages, and clans or tribes, wiping them out entirely or forcefully converting them to their ways of worshipping the "One True God." There is also a holy war raging in the Middle East today, where extreme Islamists wage battles against those that would choose democracy over theocracy, and be governed by right and wrong instead of the religious views and laws of a fanatical minority with great military might and a willingness to die for what they believe to be the "true answer."

However, every day, and in every moment of every day, we have the ability to choose our own path. We have the right to begin again, to stop doing harm to ourselves through poor decision making and to use our knowledge and common sense to seek out the truths that are real to us and applicable to our lives in the here and now. We no longer have to just accept the teachings of a few in power at the top of the religious hierarchy. We can think for ourselves, research the past for ourselves, and worship for ourselves, embracing aspects of spirituality and traditions from the past or creating new traditions that help us connect with the Creator on a greater level.

Creation

Over time, Pagans and Wiccans have embraced Creation myths from the past, sometimes adapting them to more modern times. They have also created new versions of the Creation story which can be found in many books on modern-day worship. It is largely represented in modern Wiccan tradition and ceremony that the Great Union (lovemaking/procreating) of the God and Goddess formed the Universe and everything in it. This is celebrated traditionally as Beltane, also known as May Day, which occurs the evening of April 30 and the day of May 1 each year.

For my part, I have created a couple of Creation myths for fun, one of which I will share here. The myth portion was written tongue-in-cheek as a gift to a stoner that I know and love dearly. The meditation can be done with simple breathing and visualization techniques.

The Great God exhaled . . .

And as a joyous buzz settled in, the vision began to emerge. He floated, then soared through the vastness of space and from his tie-dye cloak, trails of galaxies, suns and moons, planets and stars, all formed in his wake. Colors and shapes that had never existed came into being as he swirled and glided through the Universe. Then he paused to reflect on His creations and smiled.

One particular planet caught His eye. Small and insignificant though it seemed, there was something about it that grabbed His attention. It seemed to sparkle in space as a small sun bounced beams of light onto the surfaces of its oceans. On the other side, in perfect balance, was a moon. It reflected the light of the sun onto the satellite's surface and bathed it in a silvery glow.

He went to it then. He blew on it and the winds formed. Waves rolled and trees danced in the breeze. The sound of the surf seemed to sing to Him as He dove into the seas. He swam her shallow ponds and explored her cavernous trenches and, in His wake, all the creatures that dwell in the waters were formed. He marveled at their uniqueness and was pleased.

As He came ashore, the scent of wildflowers wafted toward Him. He walked the lands then, combing the beaches and forests, traversing the mountains and tasting the fruit of its soil. From His footprints sprang forth all the creatures that walk the Earth and fly through the Heavens. He was pleased by their beauty and diversity.

But there was still something missing. He wanted someone to share in the Glory of His creation. So he searched within and without, taking all the necessary ingredients in perfect balance, and he created Man and Woman. His passion overflowed at their creation and they, too, became as one with the Universe and made love under the heavens that He had created.

Then He spoke to them saying, "You are my children and this Earth is the Mother of All Life. She shall be called Gaia. Our seed shall be scattered throughout the lands and our children shall know it. Rejoice in Her and care for Her and you shall bring forth many future generations. This is the covenant of the Care Givers of Life, the worshippers of the Great God!"

The meditation:

In a quiet area, find a place you can safely burn a candle and some incense. Bathing or showering before meditation is not necessary but can aid in relaxation. Take a few deep cleansing breaths, picturing yourself surrounded by a soothing, white light. Clear your mind and focus on your desired goal. As you visualize, try to see in your mind's eye performing the actions that will lead to the successful completion of your goal. Once you have this vision clearly formed in your mind, picture the vision in the color that corresponds with your need. Imagine yourself completing your goal and embrace what that feels like. You may want to recognize this feeling in the future. It may present itself, along with images from this vision, as you actually journey toward your goal. Similar colors can be used in selecting a candle. Always be sure to thank the Gods for answering your prayers.

RED: love and lust, career goals, survival

ORANGE: property deals, ambition, general success

YELLOW: intelligence, accelerated learning, memory, selling yourself

PINK: romance, emotional healing, affection, friendship

GREEN: physical healing, monetary success, abundance and growth

BLUE: good fortune, wisdom, calm, reassurance, creativity

PURPLE: self-assurance, hidden knowledge, influencing people in high places

BLACK: protection, repelling negativity

WHITE: peace, purity, spirituality, a good substitute for any other color

Wiccaning

This is also the time of the year we celebrate the beginning of new life by performing a Wiccaning, a blessing for new babies that have been born since the previous year. Much like a christening, this is performed with the parent(s) and their new baby within the first year of life. We bless the newborns with gifts of individuality, to find their own path, and to help connect with the One on a real level, to find truth on whatever path they choose to embrace as they grow into adulthood. We make a promise to guard this right and to place the feet of the children on a path to spirituality where they can walk with God as they choose. This ceremony is always at the request of the parent(s). It is not required but is happily provided with perfect love and trust.

In 1997, I was honored to perform the following ritual for my nephew. This is only a part of the whole ceremony.

Invocation:

Great Mother of all, be here now! We rejoice at the birth of your Son. To us, it is a sign of the hope that the coming year will bring. As the days grow longer, may you guide and nurture us as your children, gently urging us forward on our chosen path. So Mote it be!

Sun King, Honored Child, be here now! On this, the day of your birth, renew in us the innocence of childlike wonder at the world we live in. Allow us to learn new ways while respecting the old. Take us by the hand and lead us out to play, testing our boundaries to gain new understanding. So mote it be!

Ceremony:

Gather one and all! Celebrate the Great Mother who gives birth to Him. It is the Lord of Light who is born again!

A female representative of the Goddess, or the mother of the child to be blessed, is presented to the assembled group.

Queen of the Sun, bring to us this child of promise.

A male representative of the God, or the father of the child to be blessed, is pulled from a waiting fetal position.

He who has died is alive again today! For today is the dawn of rebirth!

All join in the following chant.

King of the Sun! Life's just begun!

When chant dies down,

Priestess: The Dark God has passed the Gate. He has been reborn through the Mother and rises as the Lord of Light!

This is the season of gifts and giving. It is also a time to rejoice in the birth of new life and renewed hope. One of the most special gifts that we have received from the God and Goddess is the ability to create and continue the cycle of new life. It is the very essence of the Wheel of Life as it turns ever on.

Ask the parents to bring the child forward. The Priestess takes the child and cradles it while saying the next part.

This year, we have been blessed in such a way through the birth of this child, _____. His parents, _____ *and _____ have been given one of the greatest gifts two people can share. They have likewise been gifted a great charge, as the responsibility and commitment of parenthood is not a light burden to bear. Therefore, let them always walk with the Lord and Lady, seeking the joy and light of life and passing it on to their son. Let them be strengthened and comforted by the presence of their Creators and, in turn, strengthen and comfort their own creation!*

Return child to the parents. Smudge and anoint family.

Priestess: I bless this child in the name of the Lord and Lady. With air and fire, May he be cleansed and purified. With water and earth, may he be anointed and dedicated. May the Lord and Lady bestow upon him joy and happiness. May They protect him and keep him safe from harm and may his feet stay firmly on the Path of Light and Truth! So Mote it be!

I was similarly blessed again in 2004 when my own granddaughter was brought into this world. It was a very emotional and happy time for me, and I was honored that my son chose to place his daughter's feet on our path. While this ceremony was performed at Beltane, the theme is still the same.

Now is the time of creation, when the Universe was formed of the love that was shared between the God and Goddess. So complete was their joy in each other that all things came into being. All aspects of Nature reflect this duality. Without sorrow, there is no joy. Without pain, there is no pleasure. Without woman, there is no man. We ask the blessings of the Lord and Lady as we gather to celebrate Their creations.

As we grow and evolve, the basic truth of this duality never changes. Yet we are separate in Nature from the beasts of the field and forest, the birds in the sky and the flowers and trees. Only we have the ability to connect to the Divine through our union with each other. We experience through orgasm the ecstasy of the union of the God and Goddess. We alone, as Their children, have the right and ability to choose our partner in this union, to form long lasting bonds of love and friendship that override the primal urge to simply procreate, and allow us to seek the joy that is realized in the bonding of two spirits.

Today we are blessed to gather and celebrate this union. We have chosen once again to come together in love and friendship and dance around the Maypole, symbol of our Lord's fertility. We also gather to celebrate the womb of the Lady from which all life springs.

Parents, please step forward.

In these two people, we have the perfect representation of the Lord and Lady on the Wheel of the Year. Their choice to bond emotionally and physically has created love; this love has created Life. Today we present _____, child of their union, to receive the gifts of the Divine Mother and Father.

They say it takes a village to raise a child. Today this is truer than ever. And so, surrounded by our spiritual "village," we ask for these blessings to be bestowed upon your child.

Holy water or essential oil can be used to make the religious symbol of your choice on or over each body part as it is mentioned in the ceremony.

> *Blessed be your mouth, that you shall always speak the truth with wisdom. So Mote it be.*
>
> *Blessed be your hands, that they will be creative, gentle and skillful. So Mote it be.*
>
> *Blessed be your heart, that you will give and receive love, friendship and compassion. So Mote it be.*
>
> *Blessed be your womb/sex that you may continue the cycle of life. So Mote it be.*
>
> *Blessed be your feet, that you may always walk the path of peace and enlightenment. So Mote it be.* [4]
>
> *Each of the elements represents some part of us as human beings. Let us make a journey around the circle as we welcome your child into the circle of life.*

Parents and child are led around the circle to the different elements. Each elemental will introduce itself to the baby and impart a small wish for the child as well. Then they will be led back to the center of the circle.

> *Lord and Lady of the Wood, look down upon this child with grace. May their path always be illuminated as they seek You and themselves. So mote it be.*

I have also had the privilege of acting as an Elemental for other Wiccanings. Here are two Elementals for your consideration:

---

[4] A version of this 'Five-Fold Kiss' is presented in Raymond Buckland's Complete Book of Witchcraft.

Blessings be upon you, child of Water. I gift you with this Aquamarine, a stone of Water. Water lives in the direction of the West, wherein dwells the folk of Summerland, of Faerie. It is where we all go when we leave this place. Water nurtures our bodies, our minds, and our souls. It is from water that we come and our emotions are ruled by Water. Water's gifts are these; comfort, motherly love, and love of the heart. Go to the water to calm your unsettled soul. But beware! Water can flood and devastate your emotions as it can the land. Beware of sinking into your emotions. Seek balance and know that the Spirit of Water is always with you! Blessed be!

I am the Spirit of Fire. Today I live within you as a tiny spark, a mere image of the passion by which you were created. Now I rumble inside you like thunder, like the lava that flows deep within the Earth, warming and protecting, changing and forging your spirit. As you grow, may your spirit grow as well. May passion and creativity burst forth like an eruption at your beck and call. May the purging power of fire purify all that comes across your path and transform all negativity into joy. May you fly with dragon's wings through the Spiral of Life. Blessed be!

While this process is not a promise to dedicate the child to Wicca, per se, it is a promise to lead the child toward a spiritual life. By making this promise, we honor the One and give the child a solid foundation on which to build their own spiritual journey and beliefs.

Candelmas

Major Holiday—A celebration of the growing light and the returning of warmth to the Earth—February 2. Typically we gather in the evenings to celebrate and light candles, as many as we can find, to give light to the darkness. This usually takes the form of a "Festival of Brigid." In ancient Celtic tradition, she was known as the Goddess of Fire, Inspiration,

Smithcraft, Poetry, and Healing.

This is the time of year we decided to allow prospective initiates to seek admission into our group (coven). To us, there seemed to be no better time of the year than during a Celebration of Light!

The act of seeking admission into any spiritually based group is an acknowledgement of your desire to "Seek the Light" by connecting with the Divine. While your average church does not require initiation for you to be admitted on any given Sunday, Wiccans are, as a whole and by nature of experience, a more secretive and cloistered group. Adherents to this particular faith, in the present as well as the distant past of the Burning Times, circa the fourteenth to the eighteenth century, have experienced discrimination and elimination by others who did not understand their ways or who sought to take away their personal power or property. Therefore, we wish to know the intent of the person who is seeking admission into our group for reasons of safety as well as sincerity.

Those of us who gather to worship in this way have dedicated time, energy, and vulnerability to opening ourselves to the many experiences we have had within the circle. We agree to trust that anything brought into the circle, be it a tradition to explore, an idea to share, or a truth to tell, will be done so "In Perfect Love and Perfect Trust." We agree to leave behind mistrust and negativity and embrace each other as brothers and sisters in the eyes of the Creator. This complete trust fosters spiritual awareness and connectivity that can only be described as miraculous or divine, leading to true growth and enlightenment for the individuals participating in this process.

Petitioning

In our tradition, we ask that a prospective initiate verbally petition the group, stating her reasons for seeking admission, and choosing a spiritual name for herself, which will be revealed at the time of the petition. This is a magickal name by which the initiate will be known in the circle and will be kept secret, used only by the group. This is the first act of perfect love and trust that is asked of the prospective initiate. Although some adherents choose to make their magickal name common knowledge, others wish to guard their identity as witches from those who might misunderstand or discriminate against them in some aspect of their lives. Therefore, by becoming part of a coven or magickal group, you are committing to respect and protect the other participants in the group by keeping their magickal identities, and their choice of path, a secret from the "secular" world. "Outing" your fellow practitioners is one of the big No-No's of the Wiccan world.

In 1996, we held a Candelmas celebration in my living room. During this time, we had a friend that had become interested in joining our group. He had observed one of the open rituals that we occasionally held in public. He was further interested from listening to conversations that we had around that very living room on many a night of gathering as friends. My first husband, who was fond of thrift stores, had purchased a candle with a base molded out of one of those old canister ashtrays that sits next to the doors of retail shops, etc. It was 30" x 12" and it had a nylon rope as the wick. We used this as the centerpiece for our altar, placing other related items around its base. While it was a beautiful circle, and the candle lit up my living room bright as daylight, let me use this as a cautionary tale. The next day, I realized that my entire house was covered in black soot from burning such a huge candle indoors! While effect is important in any ritual, be aware of your environment and any limitations it may present.

This is only a piece of the ritual I developed for the evening and I included my friend's petition as one of the steps in the main body of the ceremony.

As always, create a sacred space by erecting an altar, smudging and anointing the space and focusing on your intent.

Surround the circle with candles (colors: White, earth; Yellow, air; Orange, fire; and Blue, water).

Call the Quarters. Light each of the four quarter candles as you do so.

Perform Invocation to Brigid (or to the God/Goddess of your choice).

Blessing—A Poem

Mother Earth awakes.
The touch of morning light,
Like a feathery kiss on the cheek at dawn, an awakening of gentle bliss,
She stirs at his caress, a smile breaks the cold of the long night.
His warmth slowly embraces, tendrils of gold remind sweetly of what is to come.
From the dreamland she returns longing to meet the new day.
They shall walk the fields together.
They shall grow, make love, bring forth new life and finally rest again together.
For as it was in the beginning, so shall it be for all time, without end.
Two halves of a whole, joined together, turning as The Wheel, forever.

Bring the pledge to the altar. Ask the initiates to announce their chosen names and to state their reason for asking admission to the circle as an initiate.

The ballot process should be secret. A unanimous vote is required for acceptance into the circle as an initiate. Voting is tallied after the ceremony. Announcement of the new member (if applicable) can be made during the feast.

The magickal working can be designed to fit the occasion or you can use one of the following techniques to create and focus energy.

Blade and Fire Meditation—Each participant will go to the four quarters, take in hand the blade there, and use it as a reflecting tool to consider the energy forces of that element.

Candle Dance—Participants light an individual taper from the center altar candle and dance around the circle. This is a good opportunity for a spiral dance if space provides. (Be sure that you use candle guards to keep hot wax from dripping on your hand, carpet, etc.)

Anytime a cone of power is raised during ritual, it is important to ground any excess energy before proceeding to the closing aspects of the ceremony. Proceed with feasting and celebration.

Oestara

Spring Equinox—Minor Holiday—when the length of the day and night are equal—between March 19 and 21, based on planetary positioning. This is a celebration of new beginnings and the greening of the planet. This is the time of the year that we "sow seeds" for new projects, new jobs, new relationships, and new growth within ourselves. It is also the time of the year that we typically perform coming of age ceremonies, initiations, and rededications.

As a parent, when practicing any faith, we raise our children to understand the tenets of our faith as we make it a part of our lives. In choosing Wicca as my path, I involved my children in almost all of our ceremonies and rituals. From a very young age, they danced, sang, feasted, and celebrated life alongside us, learning as they went the things that we held sacred and worthy of celebration. As a natural progression of that journey, the kids were given the opportunity to be the focus of a Coming of Age ceremony. The ceremonies were designed with each of them in mind but also as a general rite that could be used with other hereditary Wiccans.

We wanted to acknowledge the importance of that turning point in life when you start seeing things through adult eyes, leaving childlike things in the past to explore your existence as part of the greater human experience. Therefore, as each child approached the age of thirteen, they were asked if they wanted to have this ceremony completed for them. One of my two sons actually chose not to have this ceremony performed in his honor. I think he was not quite ready to let go of the inner child he was so closely guarding. This decision was totally his to make and was held with complete respect. We all come to decisions in our own way and time and I think he was exercising his first adult instinct in that moment. He was not sure that my path should be the one for him, and needed to make his own choice when the time came. This showed bravery! It was evident that he was on his way to becoming an individual, not conforming to what he was unsure of because of some imagined family pressure or even peer pressure, and I was a little surprised but very proud when he made his choice!

My other son chose to perform this rite and so did my daughter. During my son's ceremony, we included some activities that were decidedly male. As part of his coming of age, he was sent through a gauntlet of our male coveners wielding Nerf swords and bats, pummeling at him as he ran to the other end. The tools used for this part of the ceremony were harmless in the hands of our loving brothers, yet they served as a reminder. All of life's paths will include some lumps and bumps, some rough spots and hardships. With perseverance and courage, you can reach the end of any journey on which you embark and be victorious!

Coming of Age

In 2001, my daughter turned thirteen. As her brothers before her, she was given the opportunity to receive this ceremony and happily accepted the honor. I developed the following ceremony for her and it was truly a lovely moment in my journey as a mother and a Priestess.

This ceremony was performed by all women for my daughter, who was raised as a hereditary Witch and was coming into her Maidenhood at age thirteen. It can be adapted for a young boy coming into Manhood at the same approximate age and the candles would represent Acolyte, Father, and Sage.

Three candles representing the Maiden, Mother, and Crone are included in the list of altar items to be used in this ceremony. The circle was cast as described before in previous chapters.

Invocation:

*I call upon the Maiden, Goddess of Spring, Virgin Huntress.
By the white light of your waxing face may we be renewed.
Let youth, vigor, and the powers of seduction be ours tonight and always.*

*I call upon the Mother, Goddess of Summer, Eternal Teacher.
Under the fullness of your countenance, our blood flows red.
Let life, lust, and the powers of creation be ours tonight and always.*

*I call upon the Crone, Goddess of Winter, Wise One.
In the darkness of night, we pause to rest and reflect.
Let death and the powers of reincarnation be ours tonight and always.
May the Triple Goddess join us for this Spring Equinox celebration.
So Mote it be!*

Ceremony:

We are gathered here this evening for many reasons. We come together to celebrate Spring Equinox. It is our time of rebirth and rededication. It is the time when we plant seeds of what is to come. It is our time to look ahead, to sow carefully the plans and dreams that we want to manifest for ourselves and our world. At this time, I would like each of us to spend a few moments quietly meditating on the goals we wish to achieve in the coming year.

Allow time for each participant to meditate on seeds for the future.

May the Maiden and the Horned One hear our prayers and bless our lives with growth, happiness, and prosperity. So mote it be!

This may be directed at the group as a whole or the High Priestess may go around and anoint each person while saying the above blessing.

We are also here to welcome our sister from the innocence of childhood into the knowledge that is adulthood. Young Lady, step forward!

You come before our circle today to gain recognition as an adult. Through the years of your childhood, you have experienced many things. You have been blessed by good health and you have learned to care for yourself and others. You have become aware of the world and its many creatures. You have become aware of the vastness of space and the closeness of friends and family.

You stand before us now at the age of thirteen, a young woman. You have begun the journey of the Maiden in all her forms. You have become sister with the Moon and her cycles and have begun to understand the beauty that is the duality of man and woman. Speak to us your name, Young Maid, that we may honor you as Goddess.

The young lady is asked to have chosen a new name that will be known only within Circle. This assumes that she has already decided on her name before the ceremony. If deciding on a name is a surprise to her, give the adolescent a few moments to ponder a name.

_____ (name), today you enter both the mundane world and the realm of spirit a newborn Nymph. Come forth and meet the Triple Goddess.

A Spirit walk is taken to introduce her by her chosen name to members representing each of the Goddess forms, who will share with her some mystery that is theirs alone.

As a newfound adult, you have the right to expect certain considerations from us as your peers.

You have the right:

-To be listened to and not just heard
-To have your person and opinions respected as those of an adult
-To laugh, cry, grow, feel, and love as a young woman instead of as a child
-To not be dismissed as just another kid
-To choose your own professional and spiritual paths
-To give yourself respect, a pat on the back, and a good word once in a while
-To question, challenge, seek, and find all that life has to offer.

Along with these rights come certain responsibilities: Some of your responsibilities are:

-Respecting yourself and others
-Honesty, even when it is difficult
-Giving to those people and creatures that are less fortunate than yourself
-Continuing to grow and learn
-Sharing your knowledge with those who desire it
-Honoring your inner spirit with meditation and enlightenment
-Caring for the Earth and all its creatures to preserve it for future generations.

Do you accept these rights and responsibilities?

Petitioner responds.

Then so mote it be! May the Goddess and God smile upon you and yours for all ages, heaping blessings upon you and keeping you safe, healthy, and happy. Blessed be!

Initiation

When deciding to follow any particular path, certain tools are necessary to the practice of that faith. For Christians, this moment may be accompanied by gifting the initiate with a first Bible as a "Christian-by-choice" rather than heredity. In my tradition, we have chosen to gift initiates with all the items they will need to construct their own altar. Each person representing an Element is asked to bring one item as a gift to the newly initiated member. The Priestess and Priest also gift the practitioner with a centerpiece(s) that represents the Divine Creator(s). When the new covener has been introduced to the Elements, the God and Goddess, and to the Coven as his new, magickal self, he will have all the items necessary to construct an altar and worship as a solo practitioner on a daily basis or when away from the group. The new convener is also encouraged to bring any items that he wishes to consecrate as magickal tools and place them on the altar at this time.

In 2009, I had the distinct pleasure of initiating my daughter into the Coven of the Misty Vale. Note that this ceremony was different from her Coming of Age. The first was recognition of her right to be treated as an adult. The second was a promise on all our parts that she would be a member of the actual Coven by choice rather than heredity, and that she would learn the ways of a practitioner and/or priestess of our faith. As the High Priestess of our coven, it was my job to preside over the ceremony that we used to welcome her into our group as an adult and equal. I have included part of this ceremony here for your consideration.

At this time, I ask our initiate to step forward.

We, the members of the Coven of the Misty Vale, have offered you initiation in perfect love and perfect trust. Know that no one comes to this day without one hundred percent approval from all members of the group. So it has always been and so it shall be in the future. Do you come forth in perfect love and trust to take your place beside us as a Child of the God and Goddess?

Await a response from initiate.

Today, as you accept the Wiccan path, you embark on a future that leads into the Unknown. You choose to walk a road less traveled, to forge ahead into realms that lay beneath what is readily seen, to seek the center of yourself and all life. Know that at your center is what you seek, the light that will shine throughout the loneliest days and darkest nights, the Divine Spirit which links us all as one.

In preparation for this day, you have been asked to choose a name for yourself that will reflect the spiritual journey that you begin today. Have you chosen one? (This can be the new name chosen during the petition process or a new one that fits your role as an official initiate to the faith.)

Await response.

Then let your measure be taken.

Using cord or rope, measure from top of the head to the ground and cut. Using one end of rope, measure around the neck and tie a knot. From there, measure the waist and tie another knot. Lay the rope on the altar.

Come now with me, _____, (chosen name) and begin

your journey down the path to enlightenment.

Take initiate by the hand and lead her through the Elements.

Spirit of the North, Spirit of Earth, I present _____ (name). Show her your mysteries and bestow upon her your gifts.

Presentation made by covener of altar item representing Earth.

Spirit of the East, Spirit of Air, I present _____ (name). Show her your mysteries and bestow upon her you gifts.

Presentation of altar item representing Air.

Spirit of the South, Spirit of Fire, I present _____ (name). Show her your mysteries and bestow upon her your gifts.

Presentation of altar item representing Fire.

Spirit of the West, Spirit of Water, I present _____ (name). Show her your mysteries and bestow upon her you gifts.

Presentation of altar item representing Water.

We arrive now at the center where your journey is destined to end and begin again. Dionysus, Demeter, look down upon _____ (name) and bless her. Open the doorway to what lies beyond. Let her see the mysteries and grow more your servant. Awaken in her a renewed desire for learning and living that is in tune with all things in Nature. As she goes forth, let her inner spirit shine like a beacon so that all who meet her know the Light. As we will, So Mote It Be!

Presentation of the center altar item.

You are now one with us and the Gods!

Raise cone of power by chanting the initiate's new name. Allow for grounding before moving on.

Nature worshippers have gathered around the globe since the beginning of times. Some have called themselves Witch. In days gone by, during the Burning Times, the measure of a person was taken by the coven and kept as a means of protection. If the covener revealed the existence of the others or tried to deny that they were a part of the secret society, their measure would be brought out as proof that they, too, had worshipped in secret. In this way, they hoped that no one would reveal their practices and endanger their lives, families, or property. Many died who tried to worship in the old ways and many more have also died who were falsely accused.

In the twenty-first century, being a witch isn't punishable by death. We do this as a reminder of all those who have gone before us who have sacrificed themselves so that we may stand here today without fear and say,

"I am a child of the Goddess! I am a witch!"

Take this measure and do with it what you will. Your promise today of perfect love and trust is all the proof we need that you are our sister.

Beltane

Major Holiday—April 30 through May 1—A celebration of the Union of the God and Goddess that created the Universe, the Earth, and all living things. To many, this is the most sacred of all the Wiccan holidays and is usually accompanied by much celebration and fanfare.

In days gone by, in the Celtic tradition for instance, this celebration traditionally included a Balefire (bonfire) on the eve of May Day. This was a signal fire to the Gods that the villagers and country folk alike were honoring them with hunting, fighting, feasting, and mating. Throughout the night, they would sing and dance and call to the Gods for their blessings on the hunt and the fields and on the people themselves. Then, the following day, the men of the clan would go off on a wild boar hunt, bringing back the kill for the celebration. The victor of the hunt would then be joined with the most young, lithe, and powerful woman in the clan to preside as the God and Goddess during the Beltane celebration and to ensure a bountiful season.

In some traditions, the Lord and Lady of the Hunt would actually mate. This joining, the Great Rite, was seen as the physical embodiment of the Union of the God and Goddess, through which the entire Universe was created. It blessed the worshippers with strong children, abundant crops, and plenty of game to keep them fed throughout the year. Sometimes this mating would occur in the center of the sacred space or temple, while other times they would adjourn to a nearby tent or shelter, thus allowing for modesty and intimacy between the man and woman chosen, while still allowing some "witnesses" to overhear the act occurring. They would then send out a message that the Union was official, and the celebration could commence in earnest.

The typical celebration would include feasting on the kill from the hunt along with fresh berries, bread with spun butter, and honey wine, along with any other dishes presented by those gathered for the festivities. These may have actually been some of the first potluck dinners. There would also be maypole dancing, a phallic rite that represented the Wheel of the Year and the interwoven nature of masculine and feminine energy. They were thanking the Gods for the Universe and all its wonder.

The Great Rite

In celebration of Beltane, we have gathered many times to recreate the old ways, following patterns of celebration that were first established by our circle in the mid-nineties. We purchased a small stuffed pig that was then hidden in the bushes or trees surrounding the circle where we erected our maypole. This was for the "boar hunt" that our male circle members would be participating in. On occasion, we also used prepackaged sausage that would be cooked and eaten as part of the feast. Off to the South we would prepare a fire. It was lit at the beginning of our ceremony and fed and attended to until we finally ended our celebration later on that day. This represented the Balefire from old Celtic times and it was traditional for the "boar hunters" to return to the circle—victorious—and jump over the Balefire for good luck! It was also a means of cooking the sausages, skewered on sticks (lances), and roasting them over the fire for later consumption.

We would each choose a ribbon, the color of which corresponded to the goals we were weaving for ourselves that year, and attach them to the maypole for our subsequent dance. Then we would dig a hole and raise the maypole at the center of the circle. An altar was erected at North, keeping it a clear distance from the dancers. Flowers, bread, honey, and mead, along with a chalice, an athame, and candles would be placed on the altar for use in the passion play. We also allowed any other items that were sacred to the participants of the ritual to be placed on the altar as well.

As we gathered for the day, each participant would bring a dish to contribute to the potluck feast that was to follow the ritual, along with drums, flutes, and other instruments to provide music for the dance and subsequent party. Sometimes we also used prerecorded instrumental music or Goddess chants from tapes (yes . . . I'm that old!). Then the passion play would begin.

The men would go off into the woods in search of the "wild boar" while the women of the group were lighting the candles, spreading flower petals on the ground, or preparing the ribbons on the maypole for the dance by spreading them out on the ground around the Pole. With much hilarity at times, we would hear the men in the trees, making horn noises like they were on a fox hunt, or "stealthing" their way through the trees with their staffs held high as if they were spears, poised for the attack.

Suddenly, you would hear the victor of the hunt shout out something like,

I have captured the wild beast! Now home for the big feast!

One by one, the men would emerge from the surrounding trees with the victor holding the stuffed pig high in the air for all to see. He would be greeted by the women of the "village" as the Great Hunter and crowned King of the May (using a hand-woven daisy crown or some other adornment). At this point, if the victor was different from the year before, there would be a challenge as the new King would be addressed by the previous one, staff in hand, declaring *his* position as King of the May! A mock stag fight would ensue, where it was understood that the New King would be victorious. Then, he would take his rightful place as King of the May for that year.

To the victor go the spoils! At this time, the Maiden, Queen of the May (chosen ahead of time), would make her way to him, fawning over and flirting with him, preparing for the Great Rite that was to follow. They would then be led by the Priestess to the altar and the ceremony would begin.

Introduction

> *This is the time when wild passion joins sweet delight. We gather today to honor the Union of two into one. The young stag has reached his prime; he wanders the woods searching for his mate. She is there, ready to flower like the buds of the trees, like a blooming rose bud. The Spring Maiden and the Lord of the Waxing Year meet together in the field under the warm Sun. Their Union is complete; perfect, ecstatic, their love reaches forth to every corner of the Earth and life flourishes.*

Invocation:

> *Nymph, Seductress, Maiden of the fields,*
> *Come to us and share your love, your passion.*
> *Fill us with the newness of Spring.*
> *Allow us to grow, to conceive new ideas, to flower as your children.*
> *I call and invoke you, Aphrodite.*
> *Be here now! So Mote it be!*
>
> *Young Bull, Sower of seeds, Stag in the wild wood,*
> *Come to us and share your strength, your desire.*
> *Fill us with the energy of the hunt.*
> *Let us run through the fields in search of our heart's delight,*
> *Knowing it is just within our grasp.*
> *I call and invoke you, Hephaestus.*
> *Be here now! So Mote it be!*

The chalice is held by the Maiden while the Hunter lifts and holds high the athame. Then the blade is plunged into the chalice, and dipped three times, symbolically representing the Great Rite, the Union of the God and Goddess. The two embrace and walk forward, hand in hand, to the sound of cheers from the crowd.

Then the Priestess says,

Once more the circle of life is complete. Let us dance and celebrate.

The maypole dance is done at that time and afterward we would feast and commune with each other, sharing the happiness and joy of the day.

Hand-fasting

This is also the time of year for hand-fastings. Like a wedding, a hand-fasting is a ceremony between two or more people who wish to bond their lives together and live as one. They commit to living as spouses, sharing their lives with each other completely, loving each other completely, and trusting each other completely. In the Wiccan tradition, there are no gender boundaries that may be found in other faiths. Therefore, a hand-fasting can be for a man and woman, two men, or two women. The ceremony can also be uniquely tailored to allow multiple partners to make this promise to each other, thus creating a polygamous union. We allow for the understanding that love is universal and crosses outside of the boundaries of man's laws, and that some people have the capacity to live a life that is not governed by jealousy and possession, but rather inclusion and shared trust, love, and passion.

Typically, a hand-fasting lasts for a year and a day, at which time the involved parties can celebrate by renewing their vows. Similar to other faiths, some Priests and Priestesses of Wicca have chosen to be recognized by the government of their state as qualified to perform legal marriages within the state in which they reside. As a Priestess, I always recommend performing the hand-fasting without the paperwork, reserving that for the first anniversary of their original hand-fasting. If the couple feels at this time that they wish to make theirs a more permanent (legal) arrangement, they can then proceed with the legalities. This is also the time that a hard-parting can be performed. This is similar in concept to a divorce but usually involves less fighting, less drama, and no legal fees.

In 1993, I created a ceremony for two of my friends. My husband and I acted as the Priestess and Priest for this event. The happy couple both leaned toward Native American mythology as their primary form of worship. Therefore, this ceremony was tailored with those symbols in mind. At the beginning of the ceremony, all guests were given a candle with a hand shield and asked to light it from one of two candles, the men from the candle that represented the Goddess and women from the candle that represented the God. Then they were directed to form a circle around the altar. The bride(s) and groom(s) should be the last to enter the circle. When all have gathered, the ceremony may proceed.

On the altar:
- two feathers
- a sage stick or sweet grass
- a peace pipe (filled) and lighter
- altar bell
- two candles with which to perform the "Unity candle" portion of the ceremony
- the Unity candle
- an Indian blanket as an altar cloth

The Priestess speaks:

Brothers and Sisters, we have gathered here on this day to bear witness to the joining of these two people into one life. In order to focus all the love within us for this moment, we will join hands and share in three "Ohms."

The priestess then leads everyone in three "ohms."

The Priest speaks:

_____ and _____, *please step forward.*

Couple/Partners step forward.

Priestess: The two of you have come together on this day to form a special union, one that will last for as long as there is love to be shared.

Priest:_____ (groom), do you come to this union with all love in your heart for this woman? Do you promise to protect her space, her individuality, and her freedom, while giving of these things to yourself?

Await response.

Priestess:_____ (bride), do you come to this union with all love in your heart for this man? Do you promise to protect his space, his individuality, and his freedom, while giving all of these things to yourself?

Await response.

Then follow us as we ask the Spirits to bestow their blessings upon you.

Take the couple to the North. Light the peace pipe with the lighter and raise it to the Heavens, acknowledging the Great Spirit.

Priestess: North is the direction of the Earth, of trees, of mountains, of fields, and of home. As we smoke the sacred crop from this pipe, let your union be filled with blessings of health, stability, and harmony with Nature.

The couple, Priest, and Priestess all pass around the pipe, each taking a draw, raising it to the sky, and passing it on. The party moves to the East.

> *Priest: East is the direction of dawn and new beginnings. To the sky we look for knowledge, communication, wisdom, and understanding. May the winds carry the howl of the Wolf who cries his questions to the Full Moon for answers.*

The groom howls like a wolf; witnesses may join in the howl. The party moves to the South.

> *Priestess: South is the direction of fire, strength, passion, vitality, and life. As the mighty bear gains strength from the summer sun to endure the coming winter, may the lighting of this candle allow you two to gain strength from each other in fallow times and happy, feeling passion for life and each other.*

The couple each takes a candle in hand, lights it from the "Fire" candle, and uses it to light the Unity candle that is in the center of the altar. The party moves to the West.

> *Priest: West is the direction of water and of the Full Moon, of caring, compassion, friendship, and love. Like a wild stallion that runs free through the surf, let the blessings of love shower you like droplets from an endless ocean. As you seek love, know that the Moon has heard your howling cry and has answered.*

The bride howls in return; others may join in. All return to the center of the circle.

> *Priestess: As a symbol of not only the love that you share but the freedom of individuality that you have promised each other, you have decided to exchange feathers. With sage, salt and water, I bless these feathers as well as those who give and receive them.*

The bride and groom exchange feathers, speaking any words of their choosing at this time.

Priestess: May the Great Spirit bless this Union, that they may be healthy and happy, loving and loved, giving and sharing, and trusting of each other for as long as love shall last. So Mote it Be.

Priest: The hand-fasting cord is symbolically wrapped around the wrists of the couple who pledge their love today, representing in the physical world the bond that they have made in the Spirit World. May the Great Spirit bless this cord and those who are bound by it for as long as love shall last.

Priestess: Now that you are bound together, leap over this staff into your new life together. May the Great Spirit always make you sure-footed as you leap over the obstacles of life. Blessed Be!

Typically, the bride and groom kiss at this time.

Litha

Minor Holiday—Summer Solstice—the longest day of the year—between June 19 and 21, based on planetary positioning. This is a celebration of the power of the Sun and the Earth in full bloom.

Some who practice may argue that holidays are not for magickal workings but should only be celebrated to acknowledge and honor the Gods, giving thanks for the gifts that they have given us.

"Sabbats are for celebrating and Moons are for Magick!"

is a fairly common phrase in the magickal community. Often, people who are seriously committed to group worship will gather for all eight Sabbats as well as all thirteen Full Moons. While moon magick is certainly very powerful, especially when working with women's mysteries, the need to gather and work as a group toward common and individual goals is not necessarily the most important thing in the practice of spirituality. The personal connection that you are making with the Creator is the primary reason for practicing any faith and is the same with Wicca.

As we all can agree, sometimes the constraints of existing in the mundane world keep us busy and finding time for spirituality, or any esoteric activity, can be difficult. For most of us, work takes up more time than any other single activity. Then there's family, often a dynamic that includes fulfilling the needs of many individuals working together as a unit. We also have friends and social obligations, little league practices, laundry, grocery, cleaning, and hobbies that interest us and keep our lives from becoming too boring. With all these things "in the way," finding time to worship any faith can be a daunting task. Hopefully, it will never be looked at like a chore but, rather, something to look forward to from which you are growing and benefiting.

Therefore, we have combined the two functions on many occasions, always gathering in the spirit of thanksgiving but also performing magickal workings within the sacred space. This allows us to get a lot of work done while still allowing time for everyday life. In the summer of 2012, we had the opportunity to do a healing ritual for my mother, MoonShadow. Our goal was to harness the purging power of fire and use its energy to help localize or cast away the tumor that had formed in her abdomen. While Water is generally seen as the healing element because of its gentle way of washing away illnesses or cleansing negativity, Fire can be used to drastically purge something from your life. Its powerful, explosive energy has a way of eradicating everything in its path and lends itself to eliminating disease, addiction, and strong negative thought-forms. It also tends to work quickly and thoroughly, which is why it is always wise to heed the old adage, "If you play with fire, you might get burned!" Spells involving Fire should always be carefully planned so that the results sought are clear and concise. Muddled preparation can lead to muddled outcomes. Also, fire safety is of the utmost importance.

Healing

At this time, I felt that working with the sub-elementals would be a good way to invoke all four Elements while still using Fire as the focus of the spell.

Sub-elementals are associated with each of the four Elements and are representative of the fact that no one Element exists without the others.

The Air of Earth: fog
The Fire of Earth: ash
The Water of Earth: mud

The Fire of Air: lightning
The Water of Air: rain
The Earth of Air: hail

The Water of Fire: steam
The Earth of Fire: lava
The Air of Fire: smoke

The Earth of Water: seaweed
The Air of Water: mist
The Fire of Water: thunder

When worshipping Nature, it is always wise to use your natural surroundings and the items found there to work your magick. Plus, you get to take advantage of *conditions* in Nature as well. Remember, though, that weather is rather unpredictable, so if you are going to be outside, plan for protection from the elements in case of extreme conditions. We performed the following ritual on a bright, sunny summer day in the backyard of my home. It was ninety degrees outside and we were all sweating like hell! Working with fire in the summer presents its own unique challenges. However, I believe this ritual was effective as my mother's surgeon was able to remove 100 percent of the tumor in her stomach. Unfortunately, as I will share later in the book, this did not prevent the cancer from returning eventually.

Some things aren't meant to be and her time was coming to an end, in spite of our best wishes and efforts to the contrary.

An altar was set using a backyard fire pit as the centerpiece. Encircling it was a rope marking the edge of the sacred space that we were about to create. We placed the other altar items on the ground beside the fire pit: at the North and representing Earth, a fire-safe cauldron housing a self-starting charcoal and some cinnamon to burn; at the East and representing Air, a bundle of sage and Dragon's Blood incense with holder; at the South and representing Fire, some kindling, a red candle crafted by one of our fellow Lothlorien Elves and the statue of a red-winged dragon; and at the South representing Water, a Chalice (goblet) filled with water and mixed with salt along with a bucket of plain water.

The fire in the center was lit and participants were asked to enter the circle, one at a time, from the South. A small break had been left in the rope to allow a gate of sorts at the south end of the circle. The sage stick from the altar was lit and all who entered the circle were cleansed with its sacred smoke.

Priestess: With Fire and Air, I cleanse thee. So mote it be!

The chalice filled with salt water was also used to anoint the attendees; dipping my finger into it, I traced the sign of the pentacle on their foreheads.

Priestess: With Water and Earth, I anoint thee. So mote it be!

As each person entered the circle they were asked to walk around the fire three times, taking a spot inside the circle when their rotations had been completed.

Calling the Quarters:

Facing the West, I spoke: We call upon the Water of Fire, Steam. As it rises forth into the Heavens, it carries our need for healing. May Fire join us on this day and turn our desires into reality. So mote it be!

Taking the chalice in hand, I poured water from it into the fire, allowing steam to rise into the afternoon sky. I returned the Chalice to the altar.

Facing the North, I spoke again: We call upon the Earth of Fire with molten coals created from its very body! As it glows in the core of our fire, let it also glow within us. So mote it be!

Using a poker, I stirred the coals of the fire, causing the fire to jump in response.

Facing the East, I spoke a third time: We call upon the Air of Fire, smoke. As we smell the scent on the wind, let our minds be clear of smoke so we can see beyond the veil. So mote it be!

Using the cinnamon, I sprinkled it into the fire, causing the scent to rise into the air.

Finally, facing South, I spoke: We call upon the Fire of Fire, the unseen spark, the Sun that we celebrate this day! Burn bright, burn true. Burn away that which is unwanted. So mote it be!

Adding a small bit of kindling to the flames, I announced: The circle is cast!

Invocation:

I call upon the Goddess, Thea, Mother of Helios, Great Titan of Old! Be here on this day even as your son sacrifices Himself to the Wheel. You shall carry His light forward until He shines once more. So mote it be!

I call upon the God Helios, Sun in the Sky, Radiance and Light! At your peak you lay down your life so that we may claim the gifts of your labors. Help us see that death is only a step in the journey toward rebirth. So mote it be!

Then following a suggestion written about in *Earth Power*[5] by Scott Cunningham, we performed this spell.

> *As the intended recipient of the healing that we are asking God and Goddess for today, please take these tongs and grasp one of the coals from the fire.*

My mother grasped the tongs and pulled a coal from the fire.

> *Now, everyone, picture the coal as the tumor, burning away healthy tissue and ravaging _____'s body. Direct all of your focus on the destruction of that tumor.*

Allow some time to form the visualization.

> *Now, _____, dash the coal into the bucket of water. As the coal dies, so will the cancer.*

When the coal hit the water, it cracked and steamed. When the steaming died down from the first coal, we doused a second and a third. In Magick, there is a rule called the Power of Three: manifesting something by repeating the words or steps over and over again to reinforce your intent. The Power of Three also refers to the Law of Karma, which states that whatever you give out will return to you threefold. The third coal was the most powerful, and my mother confessed to feeling a bit light-headed and tingly after this coal had fizzled and died. As this point we paused to allow the cone of energy to dissipate, grounding into the Earth all excess energy that had created the feeling of light-headedness.

We also did some fire-gazing. This is a form of divination that is similar to daydreaming. This purposeful action helps us connect with the subconscious mind, seeking signs and symbols that may lend us insight. After some period of time had passed,

---

[5] Scott Cunningham/Copyright 1990. *Earth Power*, pg.53/ Llewellyn Publications.

we sat back and shared our visions and symbols, helping each other to interpret their possible meanings. Some find that a dream interpretation guide is helpful when practicing divination while others keep a journal of their own symbols, visions, and dreams, using references from their past experiences to shed a more individualized interpretation on their present and future dreams and divinations.

When ending ceremonies, we also follow two other traditions. We always share "One Good Thing." In our groups, we believe that each of us has at least one good thing in our lives that we can be thankful for, no matter how messed up things may seem to get. Therefore, we make a point of finding it and sharing it with the group so that we don't forget to be grateful. We also open up the circle for prayer requests, allowing anyone to bring their family, friends, loved ones, pets, or coworkers' needs to the group for healing and positive energy. The closing portion of the ritual was then performed and we celebrated together afterward.

Lughnasaad (Lammas)

Major Holiday—August 1—A celebration of the beginning of the harvest season. This celebration was originally named for the God, Lugh, who was worshipped by the Celts and the Gauls before the birth of Christ. Today, this holiday is generally dedicated to Bacchus (Dionysus), a Roman God who was worshipped between 400 BC and AD 400. Bacchus was worshipped as the God of Grape and Grain and the Lord of plenty, fullness, pleasure, and sex. He was often depicted as a jolly and rather rotund man of middle age with a goblet in one hand and a laurel wand in the other. He was dressed in a toga with a crown of grape leaves on his head and appeared to be laughing or smiling with a mischievous look on his face. In ancient times, some of his most avid followers were female and were known as the Maenads. Each year on August 1, they would hold the Bacchanalia, a celebration of food, wine, and orgy and would gather and dance naked from his temple through the streets, drinking and feasting, until at last, they chose a partner and made love with abandon, performing the Great Rite. Some evidence suggests that this may have involved the actual sacrifice of the man chosen to represent Bacchus himself.

Sometimes we just need to sit back and smell the roses. This is what Lammas is all about. Each year we look forward to Lammas as the one holiday officially reserved solely for celebration. Although we do not generally perform physical sex acts as part of the celebration, we usually have much in the way of beer and wine, representing grape and grain, and bread, cheese, apples, olives, and grapes, some of the first fruits of the Earth that present themselves as ripe and ready to harvest. We have celebrated these festivities as toga parties, as drumming and dance parties, as cookouts, and as buffets with all the trimmings.

Communion

This is also the time of year that we perform communion. You will undoubtedly notice the similarity to the Christian ceremony of the same name. This is because the early Christian priests adapted this practice from Pagan worship in order to make the transition to Christianity easier to sell to the surrounding Pagan population. As a matter of fact, many similarities exist in the various Christian observances and the Pagan traditions that preceded them.

In 2003, we performed this ritual at our celebration. In addition to the altar and central circle, we constructed a lean-to and formed a shrine to Bacchus, placing in it a loaf of bread baked in the shape of a man, a chalice with wine, and some fresh grapevines that we used to form circlets for the head of each of the participants.

The order of events was as follows:

1) Altar and Lean-to Setup

2) Blessing of the Sacred Space

3) Calling the Quarter

4) Invocation of the God and Goddess; Bacchus and the Maenads

5) Ceremony

6) Magickal Working

7) Grounding

8) Close the Circle

9) Feasting

Invocation to Bacchus:

Priestess:In this sacred place, at this sacred time, I call upon my Lord Bacchus! All is ready in the field and on the vine.
I summon you to join us for this Bacchanalia.
We shall eat of Your grain, renewing ourselves through Your sacrifice.
We shall drink of Your grape and be intoxicated,
Kneeling at Your feet in order to receive Your bounty.
Come down from your throne on Mt. Olympus and join us on this earthly plane.
So mote it Be!

A call to the Goddess may also be added to the ceremony. In this example, one would call to Venus or Flora/Fauna as another Roman archetype.

Ceremony

Priest:The time of Lammas is a time of revelry, a celebration of the beginning of the harvest. We come together on this day to recognize the seeds that have been sown and the fruit they have borne. As we look around us, we can see the apples on the trees, the grapes on the vines, and the crops swaying in the fields. These are the things that will carry us, as a people, through the long night of winter. And yet there is still work to be done. All our efforts will be wasted if we allow our luscious bounty to rot and fall to the ground. The harvest must be completed.

Just as we plant crops for food, so we plant crops in our lives. We sow seeds for the future in our minds and our hearts that we hope will grow and flourish, producing new opportunities, new feelings, or new direction. It is this personal crop that will sustain our spirit through the long night of rebirth. As with any crop, it must be harvested. Now is the time to look over the fruits of our labors and see what stands in the way of achieving our harvest. Maybe it's self-doubt, fear of the unknown, or lack of focus that stands in our way. Only through facing these obstacles will we reach our goals.

Priestess:In ancient times, the God Bacchus was worshipped by a group of devoted priestesses called the Maenads. Every year on August 1st, they would gather together and hold the Bacchanalia, a festival in his honor. They would choose a sacrifice, one who represented the embodiment of Bacchus, and crown him King of the Vine. Then they would eat of the fields, drink of the vines, and rut like the wild things in nature, holding nothing back until, at the height of their celebration, the Maenads, in a frenzy of intoxication and passion, would rend their sacrifice limb from limb, allowing his blood to flow forth onto the land, renewing the crops again until the final harvest. As he perished in the field, so too would the crops and animals that would nourish them throughout the long, dark night of winter.

Today we aren't quite as barbaric, and yet we have these symbols that represent that sacrifice. Bread, representing the bounty of the fields, formed in the shape of a man, and wine, the fruit of the vine representing the blood of the God that spills forth at his death. This will be our communion. As we each go forth and commune with the Lord Bacchus in the lean-to, we will metaphysically place our obstacles within the bread, visualizing them entering the bread and being released to the God, Bacchus. Then weave a wreath of grapevine and place it on your head. When we are together again at the altar, we will devour the bread, consuming all that stands in our way, and we will commune with the Lord, drinking of His blood in the form of wine that we may receive the fruits of our efforts.

When all participants have been to the lean-to, woven their crown of grape leaves, and pondered their individual harvest, gather again around the altar.

Priest:Take this bread. This is my body that I sacrifice for your survival. Eat of it and know that I am with you always. So mote it be!

Priest rips a hunk of bread from the "God" and eats, then passes it clockwise around the circle.

Priestess:Take this chalice. This is the blood that I have spilled on the Earth, that you may flourish in the long winter ahead and celebrate my return at Yule! So mote it be!

Priestess takes a drink from the Chalice of wine and passes it clockwise around the circle.

Priest and Priestess:Hail the harvest and Hail Bacchus!

As with any circle, energy should be grounded before closing the circle. As always, we feasted after the ceremony has been completed. On this particular day, however, there is always a bit more revelry and self-indulgence than usual.

Mabon

Minor Holiday—Autumn Equinox—when the length of the day and night are equal—between September 19 and 21, based on planetary positioning. A celebration of Thanksgiving for the bounty of the fall harvest. This is the time of year that we perform Croning/Saging ceremonies. It is also the time of the year that we hold Thanksgiving.

Croning or Saging is a rite of passage that is celebrated as a practitioner of Wiccan reaches the age of fifty to sixty. It is a recognition of the wisdom, perspective, and venerability that only comes with age and experience. While some choose not to have this rite performed on their behalf, others relish in the accomplishment of being recognized by their peers for having reached a milestone in their lives as spiritual beings. Usually this involves crowning the honored as the Crone or Sage of the group they practice with in an official ceremony. It recognizes them as a source of wisdom and advice in everything from spiritual matters to matters of the home and heart. This ceremony is widely performed by Wiccans and is a title that can be carried forward into the community denoting respect earned and given.

Croning and Saging

My mother, MoonShadow, was Croned at age fifty in 1994. It was one of the first ceremonies that we did as a group and, unfortunately, was never written down. What I remember from that event is that our circle members, each in turn, shared one important lesson they had learned from her as their friend and Priestess. She was happily treated to words of praise as each thanked her for the lessons she had taught them in their past experiences together.

Since that time I have not had the opportunity to perform another. Our next member to reach fifty decided against it; she felt that she was still too childish, too fearful, and not wise enough to gain such a title. In many ways, this was a result of not having her "Earth house" in order for a long time from a mundane perspective. It was also due to some factors that were out of her control. She suffered from post-traumatic stress disorder (PTSD) as a result of a car accident and had been trapped in a cycle of panic, nightmares, and medication, allowing life to pass her by while she stayed in her own environment, rarely venturing out where the unknowns of the world could threaten her.

Since that time, she has taken a job, opened a business as a vintage retailer, quit self-medicating with drugs and alcohol, sought counseling for her mental and emotional challenges, and made major breakthroughs in understanding her demons, breaking free from fear and the past in order to make a future that is more promising and spiritual than ever before. I am filled with pride for her and confident that when she reaches sixty, we will be performing her Croning ritual.

I have also reached the age of fifty. Although I may have reached a level of personal competence and spiritual understanding that is probably deserving of such an honor, I have not been in a hurry to have this ceremony performed. There are a few reasons for this. Through the years, my various groups have all come together for a time, learned and loved, and then, one by one, gone off to live their own lives and paths as they see fit. Therefore, my current coven consists of three members: my aforementioned friend, my daughter, and myself. I did discuss it with my friend as my fiftieth birthday approached, and decided against it. Although they are each fully capable of performing such a rite, it seemed inappropriate, vain even, for me to bother with all that pomp and circumstance for the recognition I already receive from them and in the Wiccan community as a whole. I feel that my friend is as knowledgeable about the Craft as I am and it should be her turn to be recognized first. And, in truth, I am not feeling as "old" as I think I should to be given such a lofty title. Perhaps, when I am sixty, it will be my time, too.

Thanksgiving

One of the most important lessons we can learn in our lives is gratitude. Our ability to recognize the gifts that we have received and be truly thankful for them is sometimes difficult. When dealing with everyday issues and concerns, we are often so focused on our short-term struggles that we forget to see the big picture. When you got out of bed this morning, could you do so of your own volition? Do you have all of your limbs, all your faculties, all your senses? Are you generally healthy? Do you have family, friends, a spouse or significant other with which to share your life? When was the last time you stopped and took a moment to be grateful for those things? What about your job, your car, your house or apartment? How about the fact that you could afford to go out and buy this book?

Being truly thankful is an art that must be practiced continually. I try to live by the motto, "Don't sweat the small stuff!" If we are living in the moment, and cherishing the people and things around us, it is harder to "sweat the small stuff." And when we need help with the big stuff, it makes it easier to ask for it because we haven't been burdening ourselves, our friends and family, or our Creator with the small struggles that give us character and strength. With that perspective, we can sometimes be thankful for those struggles as well. They teach us that we can overcome our obstacles and be better off for them in the end.

While we are on the subject of gratitude, let me take this moment to say,

"Thank you from the bottom of my heart for allowing me to take up your time and energy while I share my spiritual life with you."

Even if, in the end, you don't agree with my philosophies, you have spent time getting this far into the process and I thank you!

This is the time, then, that we celebrate Thanksgiving! We

gather together and give thanks for all the things that we take for granted along the way. We also give thanks for the things that we have achieved over the past year. Hopefully, if we have cared for and nurtured the personal growth "crop" that we planted in the Spring, it will be well on its way to completion and we will have begun to reap the benefits of our efforts.

In the fall of 2002, we held a Mabon celebration during which we gave thanks for the sacrifice the God made as he spilled his life blood upon the Earth, ensuring the bountiful harvest that we were reaping. This is the central portion of the ritual we did at that time.

Now is the time of the balance, when days and nights are equal. We gather to celebrate the close of the harvest season and to give our thanks for all that we have reaped. As we cut the plants from the field, we give thanks for their death, for in their death our lives will continue. Every day we eat of the fruits and grains, we drink of the waters and nectars and we are warmed by the crackling hearth.

"Not only do we harvest the fruits of the Earth, we also harvest fruits of our lives. We have cut the ideas and habits from our routines in order to make room for new insights and opportunities. We planted seeds for personal growth in the Spring and we have all reaped the rewards of our efforts in unique and individual ways. The Wheel of the Year continues to turn and we are again blessed by the Lord and Lady.

Calling Quarters:

Spirit of Air, as we enter into the long nights of fall, light our way! Allow insight and inspiration to find us as we journey through the darkness. So mote it be!

Spirit of Fire, as the sun's heat wanes into fall, light our way! Allow passion and creativity to find us as we journey through the darkness. So mote it be!

Spirit of Water, as the morning dew turns to frost in the fall, light our way! Allow friendship, love and compassion to find us as we journey through the darkness. So mote it be!

Spirit of Earth, as the harvest strips you bare this fall, light our way! Allow family and stability to find us as we journey through the darkness. So mote it be!

Inner Spirit, rest and find peace for soon the circle of life will begin anew! Allow the light of faith, hope, and joy to be a beacon to those who live in the darkness so that they too can find their way to rebirth.

Invocation:

Mother Demeter, as your sickle is raised to take the life of your Beloved, we praise you! May your swing be swift and sure, for soon your womb will be filled again by His seed!

Father Pan, as you fall to the Earth at the hands of your lover, may you rest and be revived. May your journey into the Underworld renew your spirit and strengthen you for Your rebirth in the Spring!

A "Grain Man" representing the God is made of tall grasses or corn/wheat stalks that have been shaped and tied to roughly look like a scarecrow. He is held by the High Priest and "sacrificed" during this invocation by the High Priestess. His "seeds" are then scattered about the circle.

At this time, let us each take time to offer words of thanks for all that we have reaped in our own lives this season.

We opened up the floor for each person to share something

in their lives for which they were thankful. Even those who had struggled a lot that year were able to take a moment to reflect and be grateful for some small thing in their lives. Sometimes all it takes is just a moment of reflection to help us see things more clearly.

Samhain

Major Holiday—October 31—A celebration of death, past lives, ancient wisdom and our ancestors. Samhain, or Halloween as it is most commonly known, is a time of year when we gather to celebrate the spirits of those who have gone to the Summerland before us. Just as birth is the essential beginning of each of our lives, so death is the inevitable end. Eventually all living beings cease to exist on the physical plane and the soul leaves its corporeal shell and ascends to something greater and more divine. While some may fear death, we still must realize that it is a natural part of the cycle of life. Therefore, rather than fear it, we can seek to embrace it, trying to understand its role in the world and in our lives.

While physical death is to be avoided at all costs, death is occurring all around us in a myriad of ways and is often chosen voluntarily, perhaps even subconsciously, as a means of change and transformation. In nature, this transformative power may unveil itself through a raging fire that scorches the forest and the earth, seemingly destructive in every way. But the jack pines or the mighty sequoia trees that live there, because of their very nature, cannot procreate without fire. Therefore it is this "death" that releases the seeds so that new trees will continue to grow in their place. The dusky antechinus from Africa, a rare marsupial resembling a mouse or gerbil, mates at a fevered pitch over and over again for approximately a month, and then dies of exhaustion, having completed the task of procreating the species. While I myself have said that sex would be a "good way to go," this creature is driven by DNA to do that very thing: have sex until it keels over dead. But in its fevered rush to "end it all," it has succeeded in sowing the seeds that continue its species.

Each time we make a decision to change something in our lives it requires the death of certain other aspects of our life. For instance, if you want to change jobs, you will be seeking the end, or death, of your current work environment and relationships. By taking a new job, giving birth to new opportunities, you have "laid to rest" the job of the past and moved on, taking the experiences of the former with you into the future, but leaving the actual behind. If you are in a love relationship that has become unhealthy, and you seek to free yourself from the confines of that situation, you are actively seeking to "kill" that part of your life. This may require the death of many thought patterns that exist with regard to male/female interactions, your fear of being alone, or whatever habits or personality traits you may have learned that cause you to keep making poor relationship decisions. In this way, embracing death, as a means of change and rebirth/transformation, can be an extremely good thing.

While learning to embrace death and its transformative effects, we must also acknowledge the destructive side of death as well. As human beings, we all form relationships with family and friends, coworkers and acquaintances, and we bond on some level with all of them. We are, after all, connected at the very highest level of existence, part of the Divine Spirit that is God residing within us all, and constantly connected. When one of us dies and leaves the physical world, the people who loved and respected the deceased are affected in deep, often profound, ways. While some may have lived a long and full life before their demise, others may be ripped from us all too soon, taken from us in a sudden or violent way. This is always the hardest for us to bear because the manner and timing of death does not allow the survivors to prepare to enter into the grieving process. For some, no matter the time and manner of death, an overwhelming sense of sadness is present, and for others loneliness or the sense of incompletion. Often these feelings will last for quite some time but, thankfully, begin to lessen as we heal and remember the good and happy times that we shared with the departed during their lives. In this way, they continue to live through us, not only in sharing these happy memories with others but in the lives we live as a result of having known them.

At Halloween, we celebrate those who have gone before us. We recognize the real and lasting contribution that each soul whom we come into contact with makes in our lives. We honor those that we have lost over the previous year and we honor our ancestors, whose imprint and experiences are stored in the memory of our collective consciousness and can be tapped for wisdom in the present. We also strive to gain understanding of the changes that have occurred in our lives, each a death in its own right but connected to the birth of something new and exciting to fill the void it leaves behind.

Over the years, I have celebrated Samhain in a number of ways. Obviously this is the perfect time of year to whip out your favorite costume or witch garb and wear it with pride. We have held costume parties and séances, used Ouija boards and crystal balls, and performed meditations that delved into past-life regressions. We have shared treasured memories of loved ones gone away and celebrated the wisdom they imparted to us during their time on this Earth.

One year in particular, we held our circle in the backyard of a coven member. A small shed rested in one corner of the yard and we used this as our "meditation chamber." In addition to the regular altar and bonfire, we staged the shed as a magickal space. Inside the shed, we placed a mirror opposite the door, with candles for gazing. A human skull (a good replica) was placed next to the door on a shelf. This allowed the skull to be seen clearly in the upper right-hand corner of the mirror as you gazed at your reflection. After the main portion of the ceremony, each covener made his way to the shed, where he spent several minutes gazing into the mirror, seeking visions from beyond the physical world to lend us wisdom and guidance.

Tolerance

In the fall of 2001, shortly after the attacks on the World Trade Center, the Pentagon, and Flight 93, I was working on a Halloween ritual and came upon some ideas that I thought were important to share with the group. Day after day, we were being inundated by images of the horror and devastation of those recent events. More and more I began to hear the cries for war, for justice, for vengeance. They were spreading like wildfire all around our country. We began to look at our neighbors with a little more suspicion. Muslims in the United States were being misjudged and harassed, treated as if they had personally attacked our people and our homeland.

While recognizing that this attack did come from the Muslim world, I also recognized that this act of terrorism was not an adequate measure of the believers of Islam. This act of jihad, this "holy" attack, was reticent of the holy wars perpetrated by many throughout history. Terrible crimes and torturous tactics have been inflicted upon the peoples of other beliefs and practices until the masses either capitulated or went into hiding for their own survival. As far back as 4000 BC, the Egyptians enslaved the Hebrew people and forced them to build temples to honor the gods of the Pharaohs. At the beginning of the second millennium, the King of England sent forth armies, led by the Knights of the Round Table, to convert the Moors and Pagans to Christianity while conquering Europe in the name of God. Being in the Craft, one has only to recall the Burning Times of the fourteenth to seventeenth centuries, perpetrated by the Catholic church under the guise of a proclamation known as "The Hammer of the Witches," issued by the Pope in 1484, during which hundreds of thousands were killed in the name of ridding the world of "Evil," It also reminded me of the terrible atrocities committed in the name of ethnic cleansing that occurred during World War II on the part of the German army and the Gestapo, all because one awesomely charismatic, syphilis-infected tyrant, Adolf Hitler, convinced them that they were doing the world a favor by eradicating the Jews once and for all.

But, as was the case in the events of 9/11, those decisions were made by people in positions of high religious and political stature, fueled by their greed for power and their own overzealous belief in the rightness of *their* way. These actions did not define the culture or its people as a whole. On an everyday basis, most adherents of any faith are just trying to get by as best they can, not interfering in the lives or beliefs of others but existing in cooperation without malice for those who share their communities and villages. Therefore, I felt an urge to make tolerance the message for the coming New Year.

In October, I performed this ritual. I was truly inspired by tarot cards as I struggled to find my theme that year, and it all came to me with Divine intervention while the voices of those gone before us echoed in my mind. Onto the altar I placed the Major Arcana tarot cards, the Blasted Tower, Death, and the Devil. While Arthur is not a God, per se, he is the mythological archetype of the God, being eventually slain by his own son as observed in the Wheel of the Year.

Invocation:

I call upon Arthur, King of the Realm,
Knight of Knights and Ruler of the Round Table.
Join us in our circle on this Samhain Eve.
Be our guide to the Isle of Avalon. Lead us into a place of rest and rebirth.
So mote it be!

I call upon Morgan, Queen of the Dark,
Mother of the New Lord and Triple Goddess.
Take us into Your arms and comfort us.
Take us into Your womb and nurture us.
Transform us and make us whole again.
So mote it be!

Ceremony:

"In looking for a way to center myself and begin anew, to take this time of repose and renewal to reprioritize my life and my view of the world, I went to the Tarot cards. Occasionally I do this because something so greatly occupies my thoughts or spirit that I must address it and seek insight or direction that comes from within and without; that place

where thoughts end and understanding begins. As I leafed through my deck for a significator, three cards kept jumping out at me. I pulled them from the deck and decided to delve into their deeper meanings.

"First, I began with the Blasted Tower, all too appropriate for recent times. This card represents the 'end of delusion.' It also stands for a shocking and nasty upheaval of things we have considered normal or perhaps not even considered at all. Such things as freedom of fear from harm on a grand scale, or living an open, carefree life in a society that relishes in self-achievement and gratification. We as Wicca, the wise, have even been surprised at the smallness of our world and the people in it.

"But the Tower doesn't only mean devastation. It is a chance to clear away old thought-forms and ideas, walls and habits, and make room for a new awakening. Unity of mankind; our willingness to accept, to adapt, to rebuild from the ashes of the past are all open to us as we greet the future.

"On this day, let our Spirits open to new ideas, new awareness and new life. Let the delusion of freedom become a reality in the renewal of the soul on the Isle of Avalon. So mote it be!

"Second, I considered Death. Obviously, it has been in the forefront of daily life for the last month or so. It causes us to examine our own mortality and the precious ties we have to our friends and family. I know that some of us have started an 'end of the world' corner in our garages or basements. I personally have begun to stow away small things: candles and batteries, Coleman fuel and matches, dry and canned goods. Certainly now is not the time to be a paranoid survivalist weirdo. However, readiness to face a power outage or some minor disaster of nature is responsible and something that anyone should consider when faced with our 'new view' of global vulnerability.

"However, Death also represents transformation. A new

world will emerge from the pain and uncertainty that often accompanies death. Now is the opportunity to spread a new concept of global peace and unity, a return to the simpler, valued rewards and pleasures of living in harmony with Nature and our fellow man.

"To the best of our ability, within reasonable guidelines of survival and hope, we should strive to be one with our fellow man and spread hope, peace, and faith to those in need, including ourselves. This is part of the renewal that comes with rebirth. So mote it be!

"The third card I considered was the Devil. There has been a lot of talk about evil lately, and those actions perpetrated on 9/11 were evil, no doubt! For a long time, those who have practiced alternative religions have been considered 'evil' or 'devil worshippers.' I think this card sends an interesting message to those who choose to hear. We have a unique opportunity to redefine 'evil' as it is seen by the common man. We, as the wise, have an obligation to represent ourselves and our beliefs in a way that will benefit, edify, and bring new hope and understanding to mankind in general. Although running away from home with a few hundred of your favorite hippies sounds like a great idea, now more than ever we must be part of the solution to ignorance and misunderstanding.

"Let us not be guilty of instilling or perpetrating religious persecution on those different from ourselves as was done to us in times gone by. Let us be the first to realize that all positive peoples seek to be part of the Divine Spirit which is Love. We all need each other and, in this time which is not a time, may we all be linked in recognizing evil and dispelling it. Rebirth of mankind is upon us all as a race. Let us embrace it! So mote it be!

"Please join hands.

"We call upon the ancestors, the ancients, the holders of the

Wisdom. We have journeyed far to reach the Golden Shores. We have worked, battled, and been hurt, tried, and worn. We have laughed, loved, and screamed, cried out and sang. Now we come to rest; our tasks are completed, our battles won and lost. Be our guides, our teachers, our comforters, and consolers. Come into our circle; share with us! In visions, in dreams, and in darkness, fill us with the divine knowledge of a new purpose. Speak to us in music and signs, in aspects of Nature, in inspiration and silence. Protect us with your Perfect Love and let us shine forth a Perfect Light, encircling the Earth with peace and wisdom.

"Repeat after me:

"Peace and rebirth encircle the Earth!"

Repeat until cone of power is raised and sent to the Heavens; grounding after this exercise is extremely important!

A group card reading was done for the coming year with those three cards as a base. It allowed us to gaze into Past, Present, and Future of our coven.

While the viewpoints in this ritual were tailored to the events of 9/11, the overall concept of tolerance and connectivity can be adapted for use with some thought and inspiration.

On Living and Dying

The worst way in which death can hold sway on our lives is when we quit living. You will remember that, in the chapter on Litha, I wrote about my mother and her battle with cancer. As I discuss my next point, I feel a need to go back and explain some of her life and what I think may have caused the circumstances I will relate on this topic. My mother was an only child, raised as an Air Force brat and moved around the country and the world for much of her life. Because of this, she had difficulty forming lasting relationships, mostly because as a kid they were never stationed in the same place for long enough to grow those relationships. As an adult, she tried to settle down and live the suburban lifestyle, marrying and having children, keeping house and working part time as a secretary and typesetter. At the end of her marriage to my father, however, my mom ran away from home. She simply moved out, disappeared one day, and we didn't hear from her again until the death of my grandma a year later, who died of abdominal cancer at the age of fifty-four.

My mother came home for the funeral but, within the week, had disappeared again. It would be two years until we heard from her again. During this time, she lived with my "stepdad." They traveled around the western part of the United States, making their home here and there for short times and then picking up and moving to the next city. Together they kept friends and acquaintances at arm's length, relying on each other as their only source of human interaction. But even that didn't last and, after seventeen years, my mom came back to Dayton to start over.

She enlisted the help of our family and friends and, for a time, lived a happy and healthy life, reconnecting with her children and her father and building real relationships as adults, being more friend at times than mother, but always there for us. We thought that her propensity for "running away from home" had given way to real and meaningful connections with the people in her life.

Then we lost my grandfather, my mom's father. In that moment, I think something in my mom snapped. She went into a spiral of depression from which she was never able to escape. She veiled it with money for a time. With her inheritance, she spent it on travel, on knickknacks, and on nonsense in an unsuccessful effort to bring some happiness back into her life. Then, when the money was gone, she moved in with my brother and started to become withdrawn, often spending all her time in her bedroom in front of the television or immersed in a book of adventure or fantasy while the rest of the world continued on around her. This time, when she "ran away from home," she never left her house. She continued to wake, eat, sleep, and breathe, but slowly stopped caring for herself or about life.

When she turned sixty-two, she promptly quit her job, declaring that she had worked enough in this life and she was done! She was totally interdependent on my brother and his wife for their help and didn't see that she had overstayed her welcome. She didn't contribute to the house or the family; she rather just existed and allowed them to subsidize her. Of course, that situation was bound to be trouble, and eventually, as his family grew and needed more space, she agreed to move out on her own.

And so she ran away again, this time to her home away from home, Lothlorien. After a couple of months spent there, trying to figure out what she should do next, she eventually came back to Dayton again. This time it was my turn to pick up the ball and run with it. And I did! I got her an apartment, made sure she had everything she needed to succeed, and swore to be there for her if she ever needed anything. But once she was left to live on her own, she quit living. She rarely showered or brushed her hair or teeth, she almost always sat around the place either partially or totally nude, and she almost never left the house unless she needed more cigarettes and soda pop. This time, instead of "running away from home," she ran away from life. She died right there in that little apartment, not physically but emotionally, intellectually, and spiritually until the shell that existed was not the mother, sister, friend, or High Priestess Silver MoonShadow, that I had come to know and love. It was heartbreaking to watch from the outside, begging her at times to listen to reason, to see herself with fresh eyes, to embrace the Goddess within and treat herself with love and respect. And when she had the surgery that initially removed 100 percent of her cancer, she rallied and seemed to understand for a while how important life was. She gave a great speech at Yule that year about having a second chance at life. And we, who were grateful to still have her in our lives, believed. In the end, though, there was nothing any of us could do to save her from the downward spiral that her life had become. Within six months of her homecoming, she passed away from abdominal cancer, which ravaged her body quickly and thoroughly. She didn't fight; she didn't try. She just sat there and allowed death to claim her. Even in the last moments of her physical life, she checked out, becoming catatonic as she stared off into space, not aware of her surroundings or communicating in any way. Thankfully the end came quickly for her and she didn't suffer too much, but it was still telling that in the last moments of her life she "ran away from home" one last time.

I tell you this not to gain sympathy but to make a point! The worst form of death there is comes in the form of giving up, failing to embrace the life that we are given and making every minute of it count. If we fail to reach out, to take chances, to make friends, to fall in love, to raise a family, to find careers and interests, to grow intellectually and spiritually, then we might as well be dead! What is the point of living? Life is about the journey, not the destination! Remember that it is the *doing* of life, not the watching, that is the joy. Don't run away from life. Don't run away from opportunity. Don't run away from closeness. Don't let fear dominate and control your decisions. Go forward with a giant leap of faith, balanced by intuition and heart, and embrace all that life has to offer. Every strife, every trial, every moment of indecision is a part of what makes you the person you were meant to be. And when confronted by doubt, fear, or sadness, reach out! You are not alone, no matter how solitary a life you choose to lead. Someone out there cares about you and will help, will listen, will take the time to be there when you need them. You are a child of God, you *are* God, and deserve to be happy, connected, and whole, experiencing joy, love, and transformation at the highest level.

We come then to the ceremony that I performed for my mother in May of 2013. She was so loved by all of us, not only here at home, but also at Lothlorien, that we held this ritual at the land. Most of my immediate family members, some of whom had never been to Lothlorien, along with a dear friend, loaded up and went there for the event. As per her final request, we sprinkled her ashes in the Thunder Fire that night and she is there in all aspects, whole and at peace once more. Her memory will live on in those of us who knew her, in good times and bad, and her kindness, loving nature, laughter, and wisdom will live on with us always! We are truly blessed to have shared our time on this Earth with her!

Rebirth Ceremony

Lothlorien's Lightning/Thunder Dome
Midnight, Saturday, May 25, 2013

Door Guards: Male family members or coveners
Smudge and Anoint: Female family members or coveners
Quarters: To Be Determined
Goddesses: To Be Determined
Priestess: Peacock

All members should wear purple in some form to honor the deceased. (Purple was my mom's favorite color!)

Altar/Lightning Shrine:
- Maypole at center, ribbons dangling in the wind
- Land Stones used to build platform: Purple Pillar Candle, Hyacinth flowers, items taken from her altar box/home, three "torches"
- Music in the background: MoonShadow—Cat Stevens, Drummers

Introduction:

Tonight we gather at the Witching hour to honor and celebrate the life of our sister, MoonShadow. We thank you all for attending and sharing your love of her with all who come here. We will begin this night with a ritual designed for her, and performed using her altar tools and including references to some of her favorite places. At the conclusion of the ritual, we will be proceeding to the Thunder Dome where her ashes will be scattered into the fire pit. Let the ceremony begin!

Ring bells

Air:

We call upon the powers of Air, the soft breezes and the mighty gales!
We call upon the eagles that soar through her Colorado mountain peaks!
We call upon the fairies and the songbirds in the heavens!
Sing a song of Joy, for tonight MoonShadow is with the Ancestors, sharing in our song!
For her, all questions are answered, all dreams manifest, all worries gone. We ask for your presence in this circle of love and remembrance. So mote it be!

Fire:

We call upon the powers of Fire, the creative spark and the consuming wildfire!
We call upon the hooves of Mustangs to spark upon the roads less traveled.
We call upon the fires around which we spin a tail of rebirth.
Dance with passion and freedom, for tonight MoonShadow has found renewal in the Summerland!
For her all pathways are illuminated, all passions creation! We ask for your presence in this circle of love and remembrance! So mote it be!

Water:

We call upon the powers of Water, the flowing streams and the crashing tide.
We call upon the playing dolphins and the whales in the Newfoundland waters.
We call upon the love that friendship and sisterhood bring.

Heal those who come here to honor and celebrate MoonShadow, for tonight her loves surrounds us all! We ask for your presence in this circle of love and remembrance. So mote it be!

Earth:

We call upon the powers of Earth, the primeval forests and deepest of caverns.
We call upon the Grizzly Bears and Great Turtles that dwell in safe places.
We call upon the guardians of the hearth, Mothers and Grandmothers. Lend us your nurturing ways.
Hold us in your tender embrace, for tonight we know that MoonShadow is Home at last in the womb of the Mother. We ask for your presence in this circle of love and remembrance.
So mote it be!

Invocation:

We call upon the Goddess, Hecate, Matron of Wanderers. Light the paths of awareness!
Light the paths of creativity!
Light the paths of understanding!
Light the paths of connectivity!
We ask for your presence here in this circle of love and remembrance.
So mote it be!

Priestess: Please take the hand of the person standing next to you.

Tonight we remember your daughter, Lyla "MoonShadow" Stahl. She entered this world as an only child and in her lifetime became more than the sum of her single existence. She was different things to different people: Great Grandmother, Grandmother, Mother, and Wife, World Traveler, High Priestess, Advisor, Confidant, Sister and Friend! She placed her feet on the path of life and traveled its roads with curiosity, with reverence for her fellow creatures, with an open heart and spirit. As for all of us, her path was unclear at times, dark and uncertain, but she called on her faith to get past the fear and pain, to make her strong and get her through. She loved life and she loved all of you!

Hecate! We call you!

Maiden(first Goddess appears),Mother(second Goddess appears),and Crone(third Goddess appears),we beseech you on this night! Enlighten our paths! Show us a way to honor her in deed and in spirit! So mote it be!

As we circumnavigate the Wheel of Life, show us signs! Tell us what we need to know!

Priestess will lead everyone into a Spiral Dance, taking them past each Goddess.

The Maiden will repeat the wordLive, Live, Live!
The Mother will repeat the wordLove, Love, Love!
The Crone will repeat the word Laugh, Laugh, Laugh!

Priestess leads chantLive, Love, Laughas dance progresses. Drummers' beat gains frenzy and then crescendos.

Priestess then says.

Now our hearts know the way. Let Her Spirit guide our feet! Let us dance to the Fire where all ashes rise like a phoenix to live again!

Procession to the Dome will occur at this time. Priestess will go to the main fire pit, raise the urn to the heavens, and then disperse ashes into the Fire.

Rejoice! MoonShadow's soul is free! Her Spirit smiles down on us All! Blessed Be!

Dancing can begin if room allows.

Oddly, and with much hilarity on my mother's part I'm sure, it poured rain the evening of her ceremony, and we wound up doing the first portion under the cover of the Long Hall roof. Yet, as we concluded, the skies cleared and we were able to process down to the Thunder Dome and sprinkle her ashes in the fire while remaining dry. Then we danced around the bonfire with abandon, her image in our hearts, minds, and spirits!

Life Lessons—Honing the Craft

As I stated earlier in the book, most Wiccans feel that "Holidays are for celebrating and Moons are for Magick!" All of the holidays I described in the last section of this book are considered Sun holidays. This is to say that they honor the life cycle of the God from infancy through adolescence, into adulthood and old age, and finally unto his demise and subsequent rebirth at Yule the following year. This journey mirrors the one that each of us will make in our lifetime on a physical level. We will be born, mature as we age, grow old, and die, after which we will be reborn as spirit and, some believe, to this world again. This is happening in the conscious world in the real time of our existence and is therefore "in the light of day" in terms of logic and action. That is why holidays are considered Sun events, and the Sun is the symbol of the God.

Moon Magick

During this cycle the Goddess is ever-present, changing form from Maiden to Mother, from Mother to Crone, and back again to Maiden without her life cycle ever coming to an end. She represents the unwavering constant of the Universe and of energy itself, and of that which is the Divine. The Goddess' symbol, therefore, is the Moon. She is the revealer of mysteries and things hidden from view. Just as the Moon illuminates what cannot been seen in the light of day, so does the Goddess reveal the inner workings of our subconscious and the desires of our hearts. To enhance our ability to tap into our whole consciousness and into the Divine itself, we can look to the Moon as an amplifier of our magickal intent.

The Moon becomes full every twenty-eight to twenty-nine days, a total of thirteen times over the course of the calendar year. In Native American mythology, each Moon has a name that corresponds to the month during which it is full. These names are as follows:

- Wolf Moon: January—Amid the cold and deep snows of midwinter, the wolf packs howled hungrily outside Indian villages; thus, the name for January's full Moon. Sometimes it was also referred to as the Old Moon, or the Moon after Yule. Some called it the Snow Moon, but most tribes applied that name to the next Moon.

- Snow Moon: February—Since the heaviest snow usually falls during this month, native tribes of the north and east most often called February's full Moon the Snow Moon. Some tribes also referred to this Moon as the Hunger Moon, since harsh weather conditions in their areas made hunting very difficult and stores may be running low.

- Worm Moon: March—As the temperature begins to warm and the ground begins to thaw, earthworm casts appear, heralding the return of the robins. The more northern tribes knew this Moon as the Crow Moon, when the cawing of crows signaled the end of winter; or the Crust Moon, because the snow cover becomes crusted from thawing by day and freezing at night. The Sap Moon, marking the time of tapping maple trees, is another variation. To the settlers, it was also known as the Lenten Moon, and was considered to be the last full Moon of winter.

- Pink Moon: April—This name came from the herb moss pink, or wild ground phlox, which is one of the earliest widespread flowers of the spring. Other names for this month's celestial body include the Sprouting Grass Moon, the Egg Moon, and among coastal tribes the Fish Moon, because this was the time that the shad swam upstream to spawn.

- Flower Moon: May—In most areas, flowers are abundant everywhere during this time; thus, the name of this Moon. Other names include the Corn Planting Moon, or the Milk Moon.

- Strawberry Moon: June—This name was universal to every Algonquin tribe. However, in Europe they called it the Rose Moon. Also, because the relatively short season for harvesting strawberries comes each year during the month of June, the full Moon that occurs during that month was christened for the strawberry!

- Buck Moon: July—July is normally the month when the new antlers of bucks push out from their foreheads in coatings of velvety fur. It was also often called the Thunder Moon, for the reason that thunderstorms are most frequent during this time. Another name for this month's Moon was the Hay Moon.

- Sturgeon Moon: August—The fishing tribes are given credit for the naming of this Moon, since sturgeon, a large fish of the Great Lakes and other major bodies of water, were most readily caught during this month. A few tribes knew it as the Red Moon because, as the Moon rises, it appears reddish through the sultry haze. It was also called the Green Corn Moon or Grain Moon.

- Corn Moon or Harvest Moon: September—This full Moon's name is attributed to Native Americans because it marked when corn was supposed to be harvested. Most often, the September full moon is actually the Harvest Moon, which is the full Moon that occurs closest to the autumn equinox. In two years out of three, the Harvest Moon comes in September, but in some years it occurs in October. At the peak of harvest, farmers can work late into the night by the light of this Moon. Usually the full

Moon rises an average of fifty minutes later each night, but for the few nights around the Harvest Moon, the Moon seems to rise at nearly the same time each night: just twenty-five to thirty minutes later across the United States, and only ten to twenty minutes later for much of Canada and Europe. Corn, pumpkins, squash, beans, and wild rice, the chief Indian staples, are now ready for gathering.

- Hunter's Moon or Harvest Moon: October—This full Moon is often referred to as the Hunter's Moon, Blood Moon, or Sanguine Moon. Many moons ago, Native Americans named this bright Moon for obvious reasons. The leaves are falling from trees, the deer are fattened, and it's time to begin storing up meat for the long winter ahead. Because the fields were traditionally reaped in late September or early October, hunters could easily see deer, fox, and other animals that came out to glean from the fallen grains. Probably because of the threat of winter looming close, the Hunter's Moon is generally accorded with special honor, historically serving as an important feast day in both Western Europe and among many Native American tribes.

- Beaver Moon: November—This was the time to set beaver traps before the swamps froze, to ensure a supply of warm winter furs. Another interpretation suggests that the name Beaver Moon comes from the fact that the beavers are now actively preparing for winter. It is sometimes also referred to as the Frosty Moon.

- Cold Moon or the Long Night Moon: December—During this month the winter cold fastens its grip, and nights are at their longest and darkest. It is also sometimes called the Moon before Yule. The term Long Night Moon is a doubly appropriate name because the midwinter night is indeed long, and because the Moon is above the horizon for a long time. The midwinter full Moon has a high trajectory across the sky because it is opposite a low Sun.6

There is also a Blue moon each year and is defined as the second full Moon to appear in a single month. This thirteenth Moon usually occurs once each year, but can appear twice in a year where there are *two* instances of double full Moons in a month, once in January and once in December. When appropriate, working with the general meanings of each of these moons will serve to align you with Nature as closely as possible when performing magick.

Typically, witches gather to work magick during a Full Moon, when the Goddess is at the height of her power. However, the moon has four distinct phases: waxing, full, waning, and dark moon. Each phase is an appropriate time to do magick, depending on the desired goal of the spell you are casting. When trying to bring something new into your life, using the New Moon as a starting point for a spell that would manifest within one month's time would be advantageous. As the moon becomes fuller with each passing night, you will be able to see the progress of its journey. Using it as an astral symbol, it works to trigger the subconscious into action, allowing us to see things in new ways and make decisions or choices in real time that will benefit our goals.

When trying to achieve maximum, immediate, or timely results of a spell or prayer, working with the Full Moon is always desirable. This aspect of the moon is said to be the most powerful, as it represents the Goddess in all her power! Healing, fertility, and abundance would all be appropriate spells to cast under a Full Moon. Remember that the Universe is an endlessly abundant place and that God/dess wants us to live a life that is full, rich, and happy. When asking for things to manifest in our lives, we can't be shy or self-doubting. We must state our intentions or

---

6 http://farmersalmanac.com/full-moon-names/:June 20, 2015/ 8:29a.m.

desired goals to the Creator with thanks and confidence that our prayers are being heard and answered.

Working with the waxing moon, or New Moon, can be beneficial when starting new projects, beginning a new relationship, or trying to form new habits. Setting intentions is one of the important steps in all magickal endeavors. Be sure that you are focused on the steps that you will take to make your desire grow or progress. Picturing the outcome in your mind with clarity and confidence, clearly state your goals and the end result you desire. Give your faith to the God/dess and They will guide you in the right direction.

Working with the waning moon is useful when trying to eliminate negative habits or thought-forms from our lives or routine. It is also good if we are trying to end a relationship in a way that is gentle and does the least amount of emotional damage to us as well as others involved. In a more drastic way, then, working with the dark moon is a way to banish things from our lives powerfully and permanently. It taps into the hidden power of the Goddess, who is always there, even if not visible in the night sky. When dealing with addiction, abuse, or threat of physical harm to our loved ones or us, spells of protection and justice can be performed. One note of caution I will share is that intent is crucial when working with dark moon energy. If we seek justice in a situation involving abuse, for instance, our outward behavior needs to mirror that of our magickal intent. If we ourselves are abusive of the people that we love, either physically or emotionally, consciously or not, we open up the Universe to dealing out justice to us as well as the target of our magick. Intent is the glue that binds the spoken word and deed to the magick that is being requested. We need to make sure that our intent is selfless and true, clearly defined and directional in nature, in order to achieve maximum results.

Although I have found over the years that it is more practical in a modern world to combine Magick with celebration, I have done many moon rituals in my twenty-five years as a worshipper and Priestess of Wicca. I was pleased once to hold a traditional tea ceremony dedicated to the Japanese Goddess, Amaterasu, on a beautiful August evening. We illuminated the backyard with paper lanterns and served tea on the grass under the Full Moon, using the tea leaves to do readings for each other after the tea had been consumed. This provided some interesting hints into upcoming events that were eventually revealed more clearly as a result of a cosmic "heads up," so to speak. I have also done healing rituals, fertility magick, astral projections, vision questing, past life regression work, and banishment, all with some or total success. Other full moon events included a lunar eclipse, a ritual dedicated to raising your personal power in a group setting, and a world peace ritual at the Rainbow Gathering in Colorado in 1993. Typically, the effectiveness of the spell is tied to the intent and focus with which it is performed. However, the God/dess knows what is best for us and will often take our intent and run with it, acknowledging that we are on the right path and should continue pressing forward.

In April of 1994, our group held an open Full Moon event in the park. Our intent was threefold:

- to open our circle to the Pagan and Wiccan population in and around Dayton, Ohio,
- to generate brother/sisterhood and fellowship, allowing a broader base of resources,
- to celebrate the Full Moon and heal the Earth.

We gathered early and set up for this event with candles forming the circle where the ritual was to be held. One central altar was used. Each person calling a quarter was responsible for placement of the altar items that represented their element. Priest and Priestess were responsible for the center altar piece. A large fire was constructed in a fire-safe pit at the corner of the sacred area. Drummers were positioned around the fire. All members of the circle participated in order to give a broad base of perspectives to the event. As participants gathered, we greeted each with a hug and welcomed and invited them to mingle until the ceremony began.

Before the ritual began, all persons and tools were set in their assigned spots. Priest and Priestess began by smudging and anointing each other and the circle. Door guard and "cleanser" smudged and anointed the drummers, then took their stations at the South "gate." One member of the circle gathered the invited participants and led them to the "gate." Each was asked to declare their intention to enter the circle with love and trust in their hearts. Then they were admitted into the circle and smudged before the ceremony began.

As the Priestess, I anointed the entire group assembled, one at a time, to promote unity and focus. Then the Priest began to offer a greeting and some basic rules of etiquette. At this moment, we heard vehicles approaching from the road into the park area, and as we turned to look, we saw a fire truck, an ambulance, and a couple of police cruisers headed in our direction. Truly, we were surprised, having no idea why they would be there. But, wanting to continue the flow that had started to develop as the ceremony began, our Priest said,

We are gathered here this evening, along with the Kettering Fire and Police Departments, to celebrate the God and Goddess with this full moon ritual.

Laughter sounded, breaking the obvious tension that was hanging over the group. It allowed us to go forward with our ritual and was a great save on his part! Luckily, not all of our coven members were "in" circle, having chosen to drum and tend the fire. They were able to speak with the police and fire officers, who told us that one of the neighbors had seen flames in the trees and wanted to make sure that the park wasn't on fire. We called the Quarters and recited the invocation.

Invocation:

As the Priestess, I called to the Priest:

I ask for the presence and power of the God, Apollo. Join us as your great fiery chariot shows us how beautiful and majestic the end of the day truly is. This is the time of your adolescence. As the Earth warms to your loving touch, as the plants respond to your nurturing and protective embrace, as the shadows lengthen as happens every day, your luminescence shines upon the face of the Moon in the East. A shimmering reflection of You in the night, She follows Your path through the twilight. This is the balance of life, the light in the dark, the dark in the light.

The power has been harnessed and brought into the circle. So mote it be!

The Priest then invoked the Goddess into me, calling with a similar recitation that I unfortunately do not have in my Book of Shadows (a journal most witches keep of all their ceremonies and spells).

With the Goddess fully upon me, I felt radiant and powerful. I looked around the assembled group and smiled lovingly. Then I delivered the Charge of the Goddess, which is below. The original Charge of the Goddess was written by Doreen Valiente and is highly recognized and revered by the Wiccan community because it exemplifies what the Goddess *is* to us. I had memorized most of it prior to the event, and flowed through the assembled crowd as the Goddess incarnate, interplaying where the Spirit moved, touching some with a smile or a gentle hand, winking at others when it seemed appropriate to do so. Participants later related to me that they were also moved by this rendition of the Charge, that I seemed to embody the Goddess perfectly in that moment, from their perspective as well as my own.

Charge of the Goddess:

Whenever you have need of anything, once in the month, and better it be when the moon is full, you shall assemble in some secret place and adore the spirit of me who is Queen of all the Wise. You shall be free from slavery, and as a sign that you be free, you shall be naked in your rites. Sing, feast, dance, make music, and love, all in My presence, for Mine is the ecstasy of the spirit and Mine also is joy on earth. For My law is love unto all beings. Mine is the secret that opens upon the door of youth, and Mine is the cup of the wine of life that is the Cauldron of Cerridwen, the holy grail of immortality. I give the knowledge of the spirit eternal and beyond death I give peace and freedom and reunion with those who have gone before. Nor do I demand aught of sacrifice, for behold, I am the Mother of all living things and My love is poured upon the Earth.

I, who am the beauty of the green earth and the white moon among the stars and the mysteries of the waters, I call upon your soul to arise and come to me, for I am the soul of nature that gives life to the Universe. From me all things proceed and unto Me they must return. Let My worship be in the heart that rejoices, for behold—all acts of love and pleasure are My rituals. Let there be beauty and strength, power and compassion, honor and humility, mirth and reverence within you. And you who seek to know Me, know that your seeking and yearning will avail you not, unless you know the Mystery: for if that which you seek, you find not within yourself, you will never find it without. For behold, I have been with you from the beginning, and I am that which is attained at the end of desire."[7]

---

[7] Starhawk/Copyright 1989/The Spiral Dance: A rebirth of the Ancient Religion of the Great Goddess/pp. 102-103./Harper Collins Publishers, Inc.

Skills of the Craft

As we practice magick, there are many valuable tools that aid us in making a deeper connection with the Creator and in understanding our Divine purpose. The first of these is **manifestation of the spoken word**. When we speak our desires and intentions out loud, we bring them from the realm of imagination into the realm of the physical world. The very act of using the vocal chords, shaping the words with your mouth and uttering them aloud, creates sonic vibrations that can be received by the human ear. This moves the goal or intent from the mind, where it exists only as thought, into the physical world where it can be acted upon or influenced by outside forces. As an example, if you are attracted to someone and want to pursue them, merely thinking about it is not going to make it happen. You must engage the person on the physical plane, speaking to that person to start a relationship and making clear your intentions or desires. Otherwise, you're just a creepy stalker with issues. Although this is a very simplified example, it brings home the importance of speaking what you want into existence.

The power of **creative visualization** is another key component to performing successful magick. Let's say that you are interested in getting a new job. In addition to going through the motions of putting out resumes, going on interviews, and dressing to impress, you need to have a clear idea in your mind of exactly what it is that you are seeking. Do you picture yourself in an office setting, directing staff members, handling crises, and attending meetings? Are you more of a hands-on type, working with tools of the trade in order to complete your tasks? Are you interested in a complete career change? If so, what does that look like in your mind? Often we stifle ourselves in our own development because we fail to look ahead and see all of the steps it will take to succeed at our desired goal. Being able to visualize the outcome of a situation or goal, and then acting upon these images in the real world is how things get done!

We can also take visualization one step further. If the desired goal is to eliminate a health concern, picturing ourselves going forward in life as whole and healthy is one of the major components in the successful treatment of illness. If we are willing to take chances, embrace risk, fight for health and happiness, there is almost nothing that cannot be accomplished with visualizing the outcome and then manifesting it as a reality in our lives. Once we are willing to make a leap of faith, trusting that the Creator has our best interests at heart, and that our prayers will be answered, then healing, transformation, and Magick can and will happen!

Facing Fears

Facing our fears is also one of the keys needed to performing magick. This is probably the primary stumbling block that most people face when it comes to personal growth and development. If we are afraid of the unknown, if we are locked into a pattern or routine that is stifling or detrimental and we cannot come to grips with our own "demons," then we are destined to repeat the same mistakes over and over again. By thinking in new ways, and by facing the unknown with courage and determination, we can break old patterns, creating new opportunities and new realities for our future.

As a kid, I always loved mazes. From the simple to the mind-bogglingly complex, each has a simple symmetry and beauty all its own. They challenge you to go forward without fear of the unknown. They make you learn your way without guidance by trusting your decisions. There are no road maps to follow, no set of instructions by which to navigate. There's just you and the labyrinth waiting to be mastered so that you can move on to the next puzzle. Sometimes you even have to retrace your steps to know where you went wrong and course correct.

As an adult, I realized that my life was like a giant labyrinth and that there were many mazes within it that I had to decipher. Sometimes I recognized the mazes as lessons that I was learning, and worked with the energy as they were unfolding. Sometimes, as I worked my way through a maze of life learning, I was taken almost completely by surprise when I found myself back at the same place I started.

Take these examples into consideration:

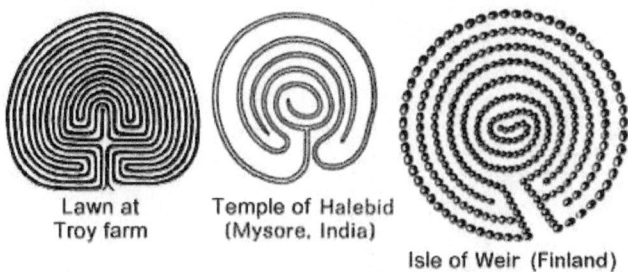

Lawn at Troy farm

Temple of Halebid (Mysore, India)

Isle of Weir (Finland)

These mazes have one thing in common. Each ends at the exact spot it begins. Many of my experiences began and ended in the same spot as well. I realized that I had learned how to "play the game" by solving the puzzle that was my life at the time. But I hadn't advanced any further because I merely returned where I started.

Sometimes, however, I recognized the mazes for what they were and was able to avoid playing the same game over and over again. Chances for growth present themselves all the time. We make choices professionally, emotionally, mentally, and spiritually every day. The key is to choose the puzzles that end in a different place from where they started. Note these examples:

After realizing the "Mystery of the Maze" I was often able to direct my thoughts and decisions in a way that progressed my life and my goals.

To try and decipher which of life's mazes are worth figuring out takes no small amount of work. Know yourself and your goals. There is no need in forcing yourself to relearn the same puzzle all over again. Learning to see the "warning signs" that you are about to repeat the same mistakes you've made in the past is one of the keys to personal growth.

In 2009, I designed this ritual to address facing our fears. Elements of all the skills that I just discussed are in this rite. It was performed at Yule and was meant to be an ongoing project for the coven to explore throughout the coming year.

We gather on this darkest day of the year to welcome the return of our God from the Summerland. As He is reborn into the world of the living, He brings the first rays of light and hope back to the Earth. Each day as He grows in strength so, too, will the sun's light. This is our sign that the wheel is turning and life will spring forth once more. Today we praise He who is the new born babe, filled with endless possibilities for a lifetime of dreams yet to be realized.

Invocation:

Horned One, we beg Your presence in our circle.
As the days grow longer, let the sun be a reminder that You are ever with us.
Shine down on us and illuminate our spirits.
Shine through us that we may be a source of illumination and inspiration to others.
Light the path before us so our feet may clearly find the road ahead.
Light the depths of our hearts so we may know love and compassion.
Light the corners of our minds so that we may know enlightenment.
Light the darkness of our soul so that we may feed the fires of creation.
May we go forth unafraid of the Mysteries of Life and the Universe.
So mote it be!

Eternal Mother, She who bears the Light of the World, we beg Your presence in our circle.
As the days grow longer, hold us safely in Your arms through the long winter.
Care for us, love and nurture us, and sustain us within Your loving embrace.
Let we, who are You within and without, be a source of love and nurturing to those whose lives we touch.
May we honor Your name and be ever thankful for the gifts that You have bestowed on us. So mote it be!

Today we share the first spark of creation. By speaking our dreams, by naming them, we bring them out of the realm of imagination and into reality. We give them power on this plane of existence and set our feet on the path to seeing them completed. Let us each in turn put a name to that which we will manifest in our lives during this turn of the wheel.

Each covener will come forth and name the goal they have for the new year. Then she will light an appropriately colored candle to represent the spark of creation that will grow to manifestation and place it on the altar. We will chant the name of the goal to raise it to the heavens.

As I have been reading, I came across a passage which held an important idea that I would like to share. In the novel The Mists of Avalon, *Morgaine says,*

"Perhaps mankind must have a time of darkness so that we will one day again know what a blessing is the light."

It struck me as I read this that the time of spiritual darkness for mankind is at an end. We are the beginning, the children of a New Age in which the oneness of mankind will be realized. Year after year we gather to share our dreams for the future and often they remain the same because we fail to make the sacrifices necessary for our own growth. We can no longer remain in the comfort of ignorance, refusing enlightenment because the path is difficult. We have everything we need at our disposal but we fail to find it because we are afraid of uncovering that part of ourselves which stands in the way of manifestation. We must recognize the power of the Creator that is within us instead of seeking power from some external source.

This candle which represents the spark of new ideas also represents the light that we refuse to shine on those dark places within us that hold us back from reaching our full potential. Between now and Candelmas, we will be using this candle to illuminate that we which we would NOT see. Twice a week, I want you to set aside thirty minutes for candle gazing and meditation. During this time, we will be looking for what we have been hiding from ourselves, the thing that we have purposely ignored because we are afraid of what weakness or fear it will show.

On Candelmas, we will gather again and use the power of fire to purge that thought pattern, that old habit, that fear or regret from us once and for all. We will share with each other what we have discovered and bring it into the light that it may be banished forever as a barrier to our hopes and dreams becoming a reality. Then at the Spring Equinox we will plant the seeds for our new endeavors.

May the Gods guide us through the darkness and into the Light! So mote it be!

As usual, we ended the ceremony by thanking the God and Goddess for their presence in the circle, dismissing the elementals, and feasting as a group.

This form of ongoing or segmented magick can be used either by a solo practitioner or for a group that will meet repeatedly during the year to celebrate the holidays.

Weaving Focus

Weaving Focus is another of the tools that is useful in performing magick. Many times, as human beings, we set goals for ourselves. They may be as simple as walking for thirty minutes every day or as difficult as conquering addiction or mental illness. Unfortunately, often when we set a goal for ourselves, we find that we have failed to accomplish it. What happened along the way that interfered with completion of the task or personal advancement?

Certainly there is no lack of distractions in today's world! Electronics alone, TV, Internet, cell phones, radio, and gaming, are providing a constant "out" in terms of focusing on and achieving our goals. Instant gratification instead of working hard for what we want has become the norm. Today, we are in danger of becoming spoiled brats or attention mongers because we've grown accustomed to getting what we want, when we want it, all the time. Fast food, fast cars, fast planes, fast lifestyles have all lead to a disconnect with the satisfaction that is felt when we work hard, think hard, play hard, and pray hard. In those real-life moments, we are more fulfilled, and derive a more lasting sense of success and accomplishment than we ever could by holding our hands out and grabbing whatever falls into our grasp.

Spirituality is achieved when we work toward a better connection with the Divine and by living a lifestyle that is in harmony with the rhythms of Nature. It is gained by being present and experiencing each moment of our lives in real time. When we commit to a life that is spiritual, we commit to working hard for big results, miracles if you will. When our mind, body, and spirit are focused as one toward a goal, we are able to connect with the Power of Infinite Creation and dedicate ourselves to realizing our desired intentions with purpose and confidence.

Weaving can be done mentally, psychically, but also physically to tie the conscious mind with the subconscious, thus aligning our whole being to focus on the task or goal we wish to manifest. Maypole dancing is the most commonly recognized method of weaving magick in the Wiccan world. However, there are many ways to weave magickal intent. I happen to be a hair braider, having worked at the Ohio Renaissance Festival for several years to make "the kingdom" look and feel beautiful. I also do quite intricate hair wraps and make hair jewelry along with many other handicrafts. As I transferred this talent from the Ren Fair circuit to the larger arena of outdoor festivals, and in particular, Pagan festivals, I began to offer Magickal Braids as a service I was willing to perform at no extra charge.

This involved the recipient of the hair braid clearly stating their desired goal or intent to me as the braider. Then, as I worked to braid the plats, I would focus on the recipient's desired goal. They were instructed to close their eyes and visualize the successful achievement of the goal they had in mind. This tied the magickal intent to the physical world, weaving desire into the hair and the wearer. It provided a daily visual reminder of the recipient's goal every time they looked in the mirror, bringing their mind and spirit back to the desired result. Braiding works best when you wish to attain a goal in a short amount of time, let's say from two to four days. Hair wrapping, which is generally left in the hair for three to six months, is better for long-term goals. Beads and small jewels appropriate to the desire can also be woven in to enhance the magickal energy of the spell.

In 2001, we performed a Lammas rite that included a magickal working designed to weave focus. It was a reminder for all of us that we were still not over the "finish line" in the goals that we had set for ourselves the previous spring and to maintain our focus until we could celebrate completion at Autumn Equinox.

Quarters:

To the East we give our thanks and call Air to join our celebration. The seeds of Spring have blown near and far and now our harvest is at hand. Be here now! So mote it be!

To the South we give our thanks and call Fire to join our celebration. The sun's warm rays have shown through the long days and now our harvest is at hand. Be here now! So mote it be!

To the West we give our thanks and call Water to join our celebrations. The falling rains have quenched and refreshed us and now our harvest is at hand. Be here now! So mote it be!

To the North we give our thanks and call Earth to join our celebration. Your loving arms has held and nourished our crops and now our harvest is at hand. Be here now! So mote it be!

Invocation:

We call upon Demeter, Goddess of the Grain, join us!
In this place that is not a place, in this time that is not a time, we gather to honor You and the crops You have so bountifully provided. Be here now! So mote it be!

We call upon Bacchus, God of the Vine, join us!
In this place that is not a place, in this time that is not a time, we gather to honor You and the sacrifice You make for in Your death, our life is sustained. Be here now! So mote it be!

Ceremony:

We come together today to celebrate the beginning of the harvest. As we gaze into the fields of both our world and our lives, we can see glorious crops all around us. But now is not the time to rest and take stock. Unless we are steady in our efforts, all the riches of a carefully planted garden can die in the field or on the vine and be wasted. Therefore, let us rally together to reap our reward.

With the vines of the Grape, the symbol of our Lord Bacchus, let us weave continued energy and focus on the final harvest. Let us harness His power by weaving a circle of power for *each of us. Then we shall be able to complete our harvest and enter the winter in comfort.*

Small grapevine wreaths will be woven by each person who will focus on completion of their individual goals. Then a stick is placed in the ground for the "Phallic Ring Toss," symbolizing the Great Rite. A colored ribbon can be tied to each wreath so that it can be identified and taken home later. It also transforms easily into a Yule ornament.

Mirror Gazing

Introspection is one of the necessary requirements of any successful endeavor. Therefore, it is a valuable tool in our magickal toolbox. It allows us to see not only what is in front of us but reflections of our inner selves and the possibilities that our lives holds. Many people shy away from mirrors. Some do so because their own physical image is hard for them to see; we may have actual (or perceived) flaws and malformations can be difficult to look at sometimes. Often we are hypercritical of our own image based on societal pressures. From bullying from our peers to media-approved images of supermodel perfection that are unrealistic and unattainable for most, we form a self-image that is biased. This self-image must be readjusted from time to time and should be based on the inner beauty of our spirit, not the outer beauty of the physical self. This is an ongoing and unfortunate part of human existence. It is important to remember, however, that as humans we are all flawed, and that a book should never be judged by its cover.

Others are afraid to see beyond the physical; they shy away because who they see in the mirror is someone they don't really know or like. Every day we are given a new opportunity to reshape ourselves into the creatures that we want to be. When faced with a multitude of decisions, from what we eat and wear, to where we go, what we do, and how we interact with others, we have the chance to take a higher path. We can succumb to accepted norms, becoming robots in our own bodies, acting and feeling how we are told we should by others. This makes it difficult for us to see ourselves clearly because we really have no idea who the "real" us is. As a Divine creature, you owe it to yourself to take the time to consider what the "real" you looks like. Are you dressing for yourself or someone else? Are you making decisions that lead to your overall happiness quotient or making them because someone else thinks it is the right thing to do? Often, when we make decision with others' images or values in mind, ours get lost in the shuffle. Self-love is crucial to self-empowerment.

When seeking to improve our lives and work toward a happier, more magickal, and spiritual existence, always know that picturing ourselves as we truly are is key in taking the next step toward self-improvement and acceptance. We can make our encounters positive and uplifting for others and ourselves or we can embrace the negative aspects of every little trial and tribulation, spreading misery onto others as we go through life unhappy and unfulfilled. We are not able to affect the stereotypes, feelings, and desires of any other person. We can only control how we will deal with life's challenges.

One way to manifest change on your life for the positive is by using a mirror with which to do a daily mantra. For instance, if you are feeling down about yourself and would like to take steps toward improving your self-image, make a list of five short statements that represent your positive qualities. It may look something like this:

1.I have a great smile!

2.I am compassionate!

3.I have patience!

4. I am a good listener!

5. I am growing!

Tape the list to the mirror that you use every morning to brush your teeth. After performing any toiletry tasks that you may need to address, recite your list clearly and proudly with your nice fresh breath so that you and the Universe can hear and acknowledge it! Do this three times or until you can hear in your voice that you actually believe what you are saying. I would try this for three to four weeks at least. Eventually you will have the list memorized and it will be part of your morning routine. Don't get lazy and stop saying it out loud! It is important to take that extra step in the process. Eventually, you'll actually believe it and when you look at the list, you will think to yourself,

"Of course I am! Of course I do!"

This may seem a little silly at first, but you will be surprised how easily it can happen if you use your magickal tools. In this small exercise, we have used **creative visualization** as we imagined our new and improved selves while creating the list. We used **manifestation of the spoken word** by speaking our affirmations aloud and bringing them into the real world. We used **symbolism** in choosing the mirror as the medium for the spell, a symbol of the Full Moon and water, which is healing. We took a **leap of faith** that in doing so we would receive help from our Creator and make a real difference in our lives. All these acts align the conscious and subconscious minds into one, allowing us to connect more completely with our inner spirit and the divine. This is the essence of Magick!

Vision Questing

In the winter of 1999, as we prepared for the end of the millennium, we were fortunate to have a rare combination of events occurring simultaneously. It was called the "Millennial Moon" and was set to occur on December 22. I happened to find an article in the *Dayton Daily News*, our local paper, which described this combination of celestial events. Below is an excerpt from the article.

> *The 1999 winter solstice, the point at which the Earth's north pole is tilted away from the sun at the greatest angle, will occur at 5:44 a.m. EST on that day. Sixteen minutes later, at 6a.m., the moon's orbit will be at perigee, the point closest to Earth ... The moon will be full a few hour late at 12:31 p.m. Meanwhile, the Earth-moon system, which also swings farther and closer to the sun during the 365-day orbit, will be at perihelion, the point closest to the sun, on January 3rd. The three events—moon perigee, Earth perihelion, and a full moon—don't occur often, only once in about every 133 years."*[8]

With this foreknowledge, I worked on a Yule ritual that used the Full Moon and mirror gazing as our magickal working while also celebrating the solar holiday. While I have not included the actual steps of casting the circle and invoking the Gods and Elements, I have included the magickal working as an example of how you might go about doing one on your own. It is also a good reference on how to consecrate any sacred tool.

---

[8] Jeff Nesmith/Copyright 1999. *Dayton Daily News* – pg. 1A./Cox Publishing.

We are gathered in a place that is not a place, in a time that is not a time. Let us give honor to the Full Moon at this, not only the end of the year, but the century and the millennium. This is also the time of a lunar perigee, when the Earth and the Moon are at the closest point in their orbit in one hundred thirty-three years.

We know that our Mother watches down on us with her loving eyes. Through her we see our past and our future. On this night, we ask her to show us a glimpse of our future. There are many tools of the Moon; the mirror is one of these tools. It allows us to reflect on all aspects of our lives and spirit. Tonight we shall gaze into the mirror and see what our future holds.

Consecration of Sacred Tools

Oh, Lady of the Moon, who sees and knows all things,
We consecrate this mirror with your glowing rays,
That it might illuminate our Magick on this Yule night!

Unveil mirror and sprinkle mirror with salt and water.

Mirror of Moonlight,
Mirror of Glass,
Allow me to see whate'er shall pass!
Sweep clear the veil!
Let our Sprits sail!
Blessed Be!

Each person in the group will approach the mirror, one at a time, and sit or stand before it. With the candle or moonlight reflected in the mirror, focus on your eyes. Take a few moments to allow your second sight to work. This process may take a few minutes per person, so don't be in a big hurry to make this happen. Relax and allow any images you see to come freely. You may start to see glimpses of yourself or things that are familiar to you. Take note of any impressions you may experience. Do you smell anything or feel the wind blowing? What kind of clothing are you wearing and what are your surroundings? You may see other people with you or you may be performing some kind of job or activity. This could be a glimpse of a future experience. We will leave the circle open so that each of you can come forward when you feel you are ready.

The participants came forward, each in their own time, and performed the mirror gazing. After the ceremony was completed, as we feasted, we were able to share with each other—if the spirit moved—any vision we may have received while gazing. We also did "party like it was 1999" and it was a great celebration of light and of life!

Forgiveness

There is no human ability in the world more powerful than that of forgiveness. But forgiveness is a learned skill that is not necessarily easy to learn or to apply on a daily basis. Most creatures in the world base their fight-or-flight response on inherent and learned dangers. This includes human beings. Based on experiences of the past, living creatures learn to steer clear of certain inherent dangers present in their environment while adopting a defensive posture when presented with threats that have been previously recognized and remembered throughout their lives. For instance, if you poke a sleeping grizzly bear with a stick, the likely result will be aggression on the bear's part, either threatening or actually attacking the "poker." Similarly, a dog that is abused by its owner may develop a distrust of all humans. Striking a defensive posture, growling, and baring teeth when approached by strangers would be a natural defense to the learned stimuli that people are dangerous. The reaction of a dog that comes from a loving and safe environment, however, would naturally be that of assumed trust and comfort. This might result in the approaching stranger being licked to death, enthusiastically jumped on, and generally befriended by the animal in question. As long as the person remains passive, the animal will respond in kind.

As humans, we learn about inherent dangers from our parents. They teach us not to play with fire, to look before we cross the street, and not to approach a dog until we observe its behavior. They also teach us how to interact with people. They typically encourage us to embrace our family and friends, forming trust, closeness, and even love, for the people who are closest to us. They caution us to be wary of strangers, to observe our surroundings, and to pay attention to escalating events occurring in real time, removing ourselves from perceived or imminent danger to protect ourselves from harm or involvement. They also teach us that people aren't perfect and that forgiveness should be afforded to those who accidentally offend or hurt us.

This spirit of forgiveness can also be applied to ourselves. While forgiveness doesn't always come easily, we can learn to embrace the spirit of forgiveness and apply it appropriately in our lives. As part of the human race, we are not perfect. We will make mistakes, accidentally hurt people that we care about, and are too hard on ourselves for our weaknesses. Applying the principle of forgiveness to ourselves is sometimes more difficult than affording it to others, but that's why everyone recognizes the old saying, "we are always our own worst critic." If we can apply the spirit of forgiveness to ourselves and look objectively at how an event or situation may have occurred, then we can learn and grow as individuals instead, and are better for it in the end.

Unfortunately, sometimes we get dealt a bad hand in life and we are not taught about human imperfection and forgiveness. As with my example of the two dogs, people are also the product of their environment. They can be taught fear, mistrust, and self-deprecation without ever leaving the discomfort of their own homes. Abuse comes in many forms and all are detrimental to the human heart, mind, and spirit as well as perhaps to the body. From physical to sexual abuse, verbal abuse, and emotional abuse, there seems to be no limit to the imagination of the disturbed when it comes to torture. Often these crimes are committed by people that we are supposed to love and trust. This lends itself to development of a fight-or-flight response that is skewed toward self-preservation. It also leads to a self-image that is drastically negative. Often victims of abuse feel that they are at fault for the abuse or not worthy of existing at all. That's why some amount of mental illness and depression can be attributed to individuals being subjected to abuse as children and adults.

Throughout my life, I have been the victim of various forms of abuse. In my family, verbal abuse was a part of everyday life. Although my father has always been there to teach, help, and guide us, he did this so many times by pointing out our flaws instead of celebrating our victories. While he only became physically abusive once or twice, he was never shy with name calling or the verbal "bash." He also has a voice that can literally be heard four doors down the block. Our relationship has not always been healthy for me, and I am positive that he will read these words and not understand why I feel the way I do. But I also love and respect my dad for all the love he had for us, the lessons he taught us, and the sacrifices I know he made for me and my siblings, then and now.

Then there was the bullying. From the time I set foot in school, I was picked on, beat up, and ostracized. Close friendships were almost impossible to form and I didn't have many boyfriends because anyone that dated me would have been picked on as a "loser." As a result of this taunting, and the verbal abuse I was suffering at home, my self-perception became more and more negative as time went by. Compounding this was my mother's disappearance from our lives at a crucial time in my development as a young woman. She was always the one that was on my side and now she was gone. When I started my period, I had to go tell my dad. Humiliating at best!

I was also sexually abused. From the time I was ten—when the neighbor across the street laid his penis in my hand, straight through my teen years as various adult men tried to grope or seduce me—I was unable to get a handle on the difference between lust and love. Wow, did this cause a lot of problems in my life! Pretty soon, I thought that everyone who tried to get in my pants loved or cared about me. I blamed myself for some of it and I didn't cry out for help because I felt like it really wouldn't matter in the long run and because of fear that the authorities would break up my siblings and me, sending us into "the system" and destroying the family bonds I had so desperately tried to maintain after my mother's disappearance.

When I met my first husband at the tender age of eighteen, I thought that it was the "love to end all loves." I left my common sense behind and dove off a life ledge, forever changing the course of my destiny. During this marriage, I deferred decision making for the greater good of the family, or so I thought. But really I was just deferring the inner journey that was going to be necessary for me to heal and grow. He was also verbally abusive, mainly due to the fact that he was suffering from a total lack of self-esteem and what I like to call "Peter Pan syndrome." He never wanted to grow up! Each time he was presented with a challenge, he responded with yelling, cursing, blaming, and denial. Unfortunately, I was already used to that sort of treatment so I enabled him more than I should have, making temporary peace. But in the long term, it only made things intolerable. We eventually divorced, and I took control over my Earth, my mundane and everyday existence. From there, I worked my way out of the darkness.

During my second marriage, I suffered emotional abuse. My husband thought that he was fighting fair as long as he didn't lay a hand on you. But that wasn't necessary. He was well educated and practiced at degradation. He could lay your guts on the floor with a word, a look, or a sentence. Having also come from an abusive home, this is the way he had learned to fight. There were no examples of positive conflict resolution for him to follow. His father had been clinically insane, submitted to electroshock therapy during his childhood, and would frequently go off his meds and become delusional and violent, abusing his mother and siblings mercilessly. For him, he was trying to "fight fair." But he just didn't. He was emotionally damaged but had never reached a place where he could face his demons and forgive himself and his abusers. Although it was painful, we divorced because I couldn't force him to heal and I couldn't live with him if he didn't.

For me, one of the keys to self-healing was to forgive those who had abused me as well as forgiving myself. As I looked back at each of those people, I realized that they were dysfunctional, too. Perhaps due to their own warped and abusive childhoods, perhaps due to some chemical imbalance or mental illness, they abused because they didn't have the tools to cope with their own lives or thought patterns. Anyone who abuses is not healthy, and sometimes they can be physically dangerous or destructive. It is always best to remove yourself from any abusive situation and then see if the conflict can be resolved. Relationships can be complicated, especially when the abuser is a parent or loved one. **But never think**, if you are in an abusive situation, that you deserve the treatment you are getting or **that it is somehow your fault**. Removal from danger and harmful surroundings is your first priority!

All of us have seen victims of abuse on the news. Today it is nearly impossible to turn on the television or radio without hearing another tale of someone who was the victim of a terrible crime perpetrated by their own loved one or friend. And, in spite of claiming "the right of the people to know the truth" as their chief motivating factor, the news media and Hollywood glorify and glamorize stories of abuse all the time. I believe this has contributed to causing some amount of detachment from the struggles of others: an ability to watch the event unfold without really feeling moved to do anything about it. Still, the basic nature of mankind is caring and compassionate. Most people will help you to safety and try to provide a temporary safe haven, if only you will trust and reach out. The rest of your life can be figured out as long as it is yours to discover!

Today, I am in a healthy relationship with a loving and generous man. I have a good relationship with my father. I have a healthy self-image and I like who I see in the mirror, minus a bad hair day once in a while. But it was a long road and there were certainly pitfalls. Learning to see yourself as sacred, and to treat yourself accordingly, takes work. Facing our demons and defeating them is NOT easy! We all have self-doubt at times, and this is a good thing as long as we use that feeling to spur self-improvement. This is how we continue to grow and learn to be joyful and at peace. Always remember, YOU ARE GOD/DESS! Nothing is unachievable if it is conceivable.

While some can make this journey of healing and forgiveness on their own, many seek the help of medical professionals or clergy to aid them in identifying negative thought patterns and old grudges so they can be explored and cleared away once and for all. Don't be afraid that seeking psychological counseling would make you appear crazy to others. Only you know what is happening in your head and your heart, or how it prevents the healthy you from emerging from your past. Take whatever step is necessary to heal yourself, to forgive, and to move forward.

Say this prayer before going to sleep each night, either to yourself or out loud if you are safe to do so.

Goddess, wrap me in your loving embrace and keep me safe from harm. Shine your silvery light into my darkness and give me a ray of hope.

God, build in me the strength that I need to protect myself and others from harm. Lend me your courage so that I may harness it in times of danger and doubt."

Divine Ones, foster forgiveness in my heart so that I can heal from the wrongs that have been perpetrated against me. Allow me to let go of negative thoughts and images that hinder my progress. Help me to embrace myself as a child of Creation, full of Light and Love. So mote it be!

Conclusion

During the introduction, I related that this book was something that I had to do, that the urge to sit and write my story was compelling. Allow me to explain to you in more detail why I had to write this book. Since I was a child, I have had prophetic dreams. While some might label this as astral travel, for me it is just something that has always happened. From the age of eight, I remember vividly my first experience with déjà vu. I dreamed one night that I was at summer camp, the one near our house that was the regular campground used by schools, Boy and Girl Scouts, and Camp Fire girls, of which I was one. I remember seeing a girl about my age running past a large tree that stood just outside the main barn where the dining hall was located. It was just a brief moment but when I woke, I recalled it with remarkable clarity.

Within a month of this dream, I was actually at summer camp. As I stood outside the barn near the large tree, a girl came running toward me. It was amazing how the dream popped into my head at that moment, and I was literally looking at an instant replay of it in every detail. The actual moment was as fleeting as the dream had been, but the feeling that it produced stuck with me as I grew older. At the time, I didn't know anything about the deeper, esoteric experience that is premonition. I only knew that it was remarkable!

This same pattern has continued throughout my life. I dream something, it happens. Not all my dreams are prophetic. These prophetic dreams, as I began to understand them, were leading me to the path that I was destined to walk. If I was unable to interpret the dream for some length of time, it would repeat itself over and over again. My signal, if you will, that I had chosen the right path, was the cessation of the dream. It would simply stop coming to me. When I went back to college at the age of forty, I had been having a "school dream" over and over for two years. If you have ever had this experience, or one like it, you can share in the feeling of relief that I had when the dream finally stopped, and I was able to dream about something else—random dreams with no real or apparent meaning.

Before I wrote this book, I had been having the same recurring dream for six years. It started within a year or so after the school dream had subsided and repeated incessantly. The gist of the dream was that I was commuting from my hometown to a place that represented the magickal community to me. While I typically think of the "Elves" as my magickal community, the place in my dream wasn't four hours away, like Lothlorien. It was right up the street from where I lived. It also wasn't exactly Lothlorien in form either. It was sort of a combination of a pagan gathering and renaissance festival. However, in the dream, I was living a life that was balanced between my mundane needs and my esoteric need to grow and be part of something greater than myself.

Having experienced this repetitive dreaming on numerous occasions in my past, I began to pray for purposeful dreams, asking the Gods for "just one more clue" to my destiny as I lay down to sleep at the end of each day. As time went on, these dreams started to show me symbolically that my magickal community was "right in my own backyard." I began to understand that I didn't have to go anywhere, in actuality, to reach out to the magickal community. I could continue to live my mundane life and immerse myself in my esoteric life simultaneously. In sharing these rituals and my experiences as a witch, I was doing what I was supposed to be. It became clear that my impact on the Collective Consciousness, and my ability to reach as many people as possible, was in writing my story and sharing it with the world.

During this time, I had begun to catalogue my old rituals, which were in danger of disappearing due to wear and time. It came to me then that I needed to write a book, not just for myself, but to share with others who would benefit from my experiences, the faith that I held, and the ways that I practiced it. From a real perspective, I understand this may only be for my children or my family and friends. That's fantastic! When I am gone and future generations want to know where they came from, or who I was deep inside, they can read this tale and try to imagine what it must have been like to be a witch at the turn of the twenty-first century.

I can't tell you what will happen next, but I would like to think that this will reach more people and awaken mankind as a whole to the human experience and our role in the Universe. What I can tell you is that the dream stopped about halfway through writing this book! After six years of repetitive prophetic dreaming, I am now dreaming random stuff again, awaiting the next insight to come to me in my dreams. Then my cycle of personal prophecy will begin again. For now, to type these last few words is a release of spirit that will never be diminished by any lack of recognition on a grander scale. I have completed this part of my spiritual journey and am excited to see where the next road will take me.

Until we meet in person, or in the Summerland, I hope that your journey into Wicca and individual spirituality proves to be as rewarding and fulfilling as mine continues to be.

Blessed Be!

References

Deity Exercise:

1. Encyclopedia of Gods – Michael Jordan – Facts on File Publishing – 1993.

2. The Witches God – Janet and Stewart Farrar – Phoenix Publishing – 1987.

3. The Witches Goddess – Janet and Stewart Farrar – Phoenix Publishing – 1989.

4. Myths and Symbols in Pagan Europe – H.R. Ellis Davidson – Syracuse University Press – 1988.

5. Ancient Egyptian Divination and Magic – Eleanor L. Harris – Samuel Weiser, Inc. – 1998.

6. Spiral Dance – Starhawk – Harper Collins – 1977, 1989.

7. Hawaiian Religion and Magic – Scott Cunningham – Llewellyn Publishing – 1994.

Suggested Author List

1. Starhawk – The Spiral Dance
2. Michael Jordan – Encyclopedia of the Gods
3. Silver Ravenwolf – To Ride a Silver Broomstick
4. Ann Moura – Grimoire of a Green Witch
5. Raymond Buckland – Buckland's Complete Book of Witchcraft
6. Scott Cunningham – Wicca: Guide for the Solitary Practitioner
7. Janet and Stewart Farrar – The Witches' God, The Witches' Goddess
8. Margot Adler – Drawing Down the Moon
9. Doreen Valiente – An ABC of Witchcraft
10. DJ Conway – Maiden, Mother, Crone

Resources for Abuse Victims

www.thehotline.org – National Domestic Violence Hotline website
Help offered 24 hours a day and access to more than 170 languages through interpreter services

National Domestic Violence Hotline

1-800-799-7233 (SAFE)

TTY 1-800-787-3224

nrcvd.org - The National Resource Center on Domestic Violence

Love is Respect - the National Dating Abuse Helpline

1-866-331-9474

TTY 1-866-331-8453

Text: loveis to 22522

Live chat at www.loveisrespect.org
1. For rape/sexual assault services, contact:

RAINN – the Rape Abuse Incest National Network

1-800-656-4673 (HOPE)

Secure, online private chat: https://ohl.rainn.org/online/
2. www.abuseintervention.org – Domestic Abuse Intervention Services. 1-800-747-4045
3. www.ncadv.org - The National Coalition Against Domestic Violence

Addiction Recovery Programs

1. www.aa.org – Alcoholics Anonymous. This website provides a search engine to locate an AA meeting or group near you!

2. www.na.org – Narcotics Anonymous. Same as above for people dealing with drug addiction.

3. www.gamblersanonymous.org – Gamblers Anonymous. Same as above for people dealing with a gambling addiction

4. www.recovery.org – Addiction Treatment and Recovery Resources. 1-888-319-2606

5. www.mentalhealthrehab.com – Treatment for Gambling Addiction. 1-855-717-3422

6. www.saa-recovery.org – Sex Addicts Anonymous. 1-800-477-8191

www.ingramcontent.com/pod-product-compliance
Lightning Source LLC
Chambersburg PA
CBHW021438080526
44588CB00009B/585